M000041113

BREAD ENOUGH FOR ALL

BREAD ENOUGH FOR ALL

A Day1 Guide to Life

Edited by Peter M. Wallace

Henry L. Carrigan Jr., Researcher/Writer

CHURCH
PUBLISHING
INCORPORATED

Copyright © 2020 by the Alliance for Christian Media, Inc.

All rights reserved. No part of this book may be reproduced, stored in a retrieval system, or transmitted in any form or by any means, electronic or mechanical, including photocopying, recording, or otherwise, without the written permission of the publisher.

Unless otherwise noted, the Scripture quotations are from New Revised Standard Version Bible, copyright © 1989 National Council of the Churches of Christ in the United States of America. Used by permission. All rights reserved worldwide.

The preachers whose excerpts are included in this book retain the copyright on their original work. Sermon excerpts in this book have been edited for length, clarity, consistency, and style.

Complete transcripts of the original sermons included, as well as audio files of many of them, are available on the Day1.org website.

Day1® is a registered trademark. All rights reserved.
Day1, 2715 Peachtree Road NE, Atlanta, GA 30305

Church Publishing
19 East 34th Street
New York, NY 10016

www.churchpublishing.org

Cover design by Jennifer Kopec, 2Pug Design
Typeset by Denise Hoff

A record of this book is available from the Library of Congress.

ISBN-13: 978-1-64065-319-1 (paperback)
ISBN-13: 978-1-64065-320-7 (ebook)

CONTENTS

INTRODUCTION

The Bread of Life for Your Life

"For as the rain and the snow come down from heaven,
and do not return there until they have watered the earth,
making it bring forth and sprout,
giving seed to the sower and bread to the eater,
so shall my word be that goes out from my mouth;
it shall not return to me empty,
but it shall accomplish that which I purpose,
and succeed in the thing for which I sent it."

Isaiah 55:10–11

The human soul hungers for the bread of life, the Word of God. Throughout recorded history, people have yearned to hear, read, learn, and follow the way of truth and light. And ever since he walked dusty roads with his twelve hardy yet bemused companions, the teachings of Jesus have provided life-giving spiritual sustenance for all who seek it.

God calls a diverse lot to preach and proclaim the message of love in action, to make it real and livable to their listeners. Every Sunday and throughout the week, from one corner of the earth to the other, souls gather to be fed by God's Word.

And there is bread enough for all.

For three-quarters of a century a weekly radio program has played a significant role in this life-giving phenomenon of sharing and responding to the Good News. Beginning in 1945 as *The Protestant Hour* and since 2002 as *Day1*, heard now on more than 200 radio stations, online at Day1.org, and through podcast apps, the program provides a media pulpit for outstanding preachers representing the historic Protestant denominations.[1]

---

1   See the Appendix for a brief history and overview of *The Protestant Hour* and *Day1*.

As the prophet Isaiah revealed, God's Word is not simply cast out into the void. No, it moves souls. It heals wounds. It fills hearts with love. It acts in the world. It causes change. It reverberates forever, not unlike broadcast airwaves beaming through the infinite heavens.

Day1 preachers do their best to make sure listeners not only hear God's compelling message but respond to it and put it to work in their lives.

That's the spirit in which we've put together this "*Day1* Guide to Life." It offers just a sampling of the wide range of *Protestant Hour* and *Day1* preachers representing a diversity of denominations, geographical areas, ages, years, races, and identities on a dozen important topics of faith and life that you find yourself dealing with daily.

You can use this book as a daily devotional, taking time to meditate or journal with the questions provided at the end of each topic. We encourage you to read the scripture texts included with each excerpt. You can also use this as a resource in your small study group or Sunday school class, allowing the questions and group activities to guide you into fruitful conversations about the important matters of life with the help of these trusted ministers. And it's the perfect book to share with friends and family members celebrating birthdays, graduations, or holidays, or recuperating from illness, to give them a spiritual boost.

To continue the journey, you can listen to *Day1* each week on the radio or your favorite podcast app, and find even more inspiration through our immense archives of sermons, blog posts, and video and audio resources at Day1org.

All of us at *Day1*—staff, trustees, advisory board members, and our vast host of preachers—pray that this collection of insights will inspire you to follow the way of God more passionately. And invite others to join you on the way.

The Rev. Peter M. Wallace
Executive Producer and Host, *Day1*

Day1 Listeners Affirm There Is Bread Enough for All

» "I enjoy listening to *Day1*. The sermons and interviews are a
breath of fresh air in the current political and social world."

—Topeka, Kansas

» "*Day1* is my most frequently listened to podcast. I value the good
preaching, different perspectives, and thoughtful, responsible, and
mature guidance on the Christian faith."

—Farmington, New Mexico

» "Thank you for being a part of my listening meditation each
Sunday for decades. Your staff and speakers have allowed my faith
to grow and strengthen my grace through many trials."

—via e-mail

» "God bless you for your service on the radio on Sundays for those
of us who no longer drive or have a way to get to church."

—Wymore, Nebraska

» "Congratulations to *Day1* for the longevity of this amazing
program. It's a breath of fresh air to listen to when I can't make a
church service or just need to regroup and refocus."

—Peachtree Corners, Georgia

» "Every Sunday, *Day1* gives me a message I can carry throughout
my week. Listening to the programs brings the messages alive and
speaks to my heart."

—Pittsburgh, Pennsylvania

» "There is not another program like *Day1* that gives you so many
wonderful ministers from so many denominations, and allows you
to hear the word of God from so many gifted voices."

—Minneapolis, Minnesota

» "*Day1* is a remarkable aid, not only for a fresh look at a particular
text, but as a means to challenge me in my own faith development.
I am grateful and indebted for the many and varied insights
from competent and outstanding preachers across the church
universal."

—Vernon, Texas

» "I start my Sunday worship with the *Day1* program. It prepares me for my church experience, but more than that it speaks to my heart and gives me the message I need for my Sunday school class."

—*Marietta, Georgia*

» "I commend your terrific program. It brings hope and refreshes faith in these perilous times."

—*Washington, DC*

» "Your program got me interested in church again after a long absence. It is just better than other religious radio programs."

—*via e-mail*

» "Thank you so much for making *Day1* preachers available to those near and far. It is a blessing to hear such a variety of gifted preachers from across the breadth of Protestant tradition."

—*Canada*

» "I listened to this program one Sunday morning in the midst of a load of personal, family, and professional difficulty. Thanks be to God for this wonderful message."

—*Atlanta, Georgia*

» "I very much appreciate what you guys do at *Day1* in being a mainline Protestant voice. We need your voice."

—*The Dalles, Oregon*

» "I listen to the *Day1* broadcast and read the sermons as a devotional during the week. Thank you."

—*Wisconsin*

» "I am a faithful listener of *Day1* radio. That is the way I begin my day. Always fortified with a special message as I leave the house for Sunday school and church."

—*Georgia*

1 | Life

ife—a rather big topic. It encompasses everything that makes us human beings, children of God, with the web of relationships and experiences that make us the individuals God created us to be.

There are two contradictory tensions about life that we often struggle to reconcile. On the one hand, some would say the world takes no interest in our well-being any more than it is concerned with any other creature's well-being. According to this understanding, our life is governed by natural forces over which we have no control, so the cold calculus that determines whether one individual, or even one species, lives can be brutal. As we have come to learn in recent decades, humans have little regard for taking care of the world in which they live and so compete viciously for scarce resources. The selfish and brutal nature of life means that the span of life for many, if not most, creatures is short.

On the other hand, biblical teachings promise an abundant life, filled with beauty and holy resources to ensure a life in which all needs, physical and spiritual, are met. The paradisiacal garden in Genesis and the heavenly city in Revelation give us images of the perfection and fullness of this abundant life. In the gospels, Jesus feeds those who are hungry, who are feeling firsthand the brutal nature of life.

To illustrate even more clearly that most people associate abundance with the satisfaction of physical needs, Jesus calls himself the "bread of life." Some Christians have associated abundance with material prosperity and wealth, hoarding for themselves much of the food that could feed others, and thereby creating a life that is often nasty, brutal, and short for others.

Yet the Bible affirms there is bread enough for all, in every sense of that phrase. It exhorts us to live life abundantly, recognizing our inextricable roles in the web of life around us. At the same time, Christians recognize that God has created and breathed this life into them, which means that our life, in some sense, is really not our own. So it is imperative to take care of others and the world around us, for abundance can exist only in a world in which some are not diminished for the sake of others. The loss of one species, for instance, creates a world with fewer resources and less diversity. Such losses affect all the living, even if the consequences might be imperceptible to many creatures.

How, then, do we live our lives? What elements are required to live an abundant life? What is the relationship between our daily lives in this world and the eternal life that the Bible promises? What does Jesus mean when he calls himself the "bread of life"? How do baptism and communion symbolize our abundant life?

The *Day1* preachers in this chapter provide inspiring reflections on life—and how to live it more abundantly.

"Bread Enough for All"

Diana Butler Bass • August 12, 2018 • John 6:35, 41–51

In 2016, Netflix produced a series called *Cooked*, based on food-writer Michael Pollan's book about how basic ingredients are transformed into food through the four basic elements of fire, water, earth, and air. Although the series was full of surprises regarding the history of food, it is fairly easy to imagine how fire, water, and even earth create the food of myriad human cultures. But, air? Pollan admitted at the outset that "air" as transformation is the most mysterious, perhaps the most spiritual, of all the ways in which we cook. Despite the mystery of it, "air" has also given us the most basic of all food: *bread*.

Bread was a bit of an accident—about six thousand years ago in Egypt, "some observant Egyptian must have noticed that a bowl of porridge, perhaps one off in a corner that had been neglected, was no longer quite so inert. In fact, it was hatching bubbles from its surface and slowly expanding, as if it were alive. The dull paste had somehow been inspired: the spark of life had been breathed into it. And when that strangely vibrant bowl of porridge—call it dough—was heated in an oven, it grew even larger, springing up as it trapped the expanding bubbles in an airy, yet stable, structure that resembled a sponge."[2]

With bread, everything changed. We learned how to turn grasses into food human beings could eat, store, and transport. We learned how to cultivate grains and manage fields, how to harvest and mill and leaven and bake. We created agriculture. We developed entire communities—entire civilizations—devoted to the making of bread.

No wonder that in Arabic the words *bread* and *life* are the same word. And in cultures where the words are different, *bread* is so basic that the term is often used for food in general, and later, when modern economics were born, we even nicknamed money *bread*.

And Jesus said, "I am the bread of life."

Just the day before he said these words, Jesus and the disciples had fed the multitude with only five loaves of bread. The disciples had handed Jesus those few loaves, and after they quieted the crowd, "Jesus took the loaves, and gave thanks." He probably prayed the ancient Jewish prayer traditionally used before a meal:

> *Blessed are You, Lord our God, King of the Universe,*
> *Who brings forth bread from the earth.*

The bread is broken and shared and, as the story goes, all were fed, fully fed, sated, satisfied. The disciples gathered up the leftovers, and there were twelve whole baskets of remains from the original five loaves.

Jesus's words, "I am the bread of life," fit into a larger story—Jesus has set a table on the hillside where there was little bread, and

---

2 Michael Pollan, *Cooked: A Natural History of Transformation* (New York: The Penguin Press, 2013), 207.

abundant bread appeared. There were blessings and thanks, and all were fed. This is Jesus's miracle of abundance, the echo of the manna in the wilderness, where God's people were fed real food, a food that sustained them when lost in the desert.

This is God's long dream for humankind—that we all might live without lack, that our world might not be one of scarcity, but one of abundance.

Jesus said, "I am the bread of life." And then he added, "Whoever comes to me will never be hungry, and whoever believes in me will never be thirsty." When we modern people hear those words, we think that Jesus sounds narrow, exclusive—only those who believe in this bread and eat of this bread will be saved. But that isn't the point at all. Jesus is reminding his followers that bread is for everyone. That God is the source of abundance, the One who promises that in the age to come no ruler, no Caesar would control the bread. Instead, there will be bread—bread for all, bread that will not lead to death, but abundant bread, the bread of life. Jesus tells us to pray for our *daily bread*, a radical vision if ever there was one—that bread shall be at the table, every table, every day, the gift of God.

And then, Jesus says, that age, the Age of the Bread of Life, has arrived, "For the bread of God is the one descending out of heaven and imparting life to the cosmos" (John 6:33). Bread shall no longer be a tool of empire, a product of toil, the reminder of slavery and sin. Bread will be again as it was intended, the life of the cosmos.

Bread is real food, and bread is the spiritual food of the Age to Come. In the same way that actual bread is transformed by air, so Jesus's bread is transformed by the Spirit. The bread of life *descends* from heaven; it is cooked with spiritual leaven. In another gospel, Jesus says: "The Kingdom of Heaven is like the yeast a woman used in making bread. Even though she put only a little yeast in three measures of flour, it permeated every part of the dough" (Matthew 13:33).

As an inert porridge becomes infused with life, its dough rising, so the cosmos, now sluggish in sin, are surely, slowly being yeasted. The bread of life has come, it sparks and bubbles among us, the table is set, and the blessing proclaimed. This is the wisdom of God, the miracle of

Jesus: that all will be fed, that the ills of a world based on scarcity are passing, and that the time of abundance is here.

"Life Is Short"

Brett Younger • August 7, 2004 • Luke 12:32–40

Christ calls us to amazing lives. Jesus tells the disciples to give up wanting more, share the wealth, be constantly awake for God's presence. Jesus describes a life of loving one's enemies, turning one's cheek, serving others.

God invites us to live in Christ's way, knowing that our sins are forgiven, knowing that despite what we might think of ourselves or what others might think about us, we are deeply loved by the one who created us. The value of our lives is not to be measured by our bank account, not by how we look, not by our standing in the community, not even by the amount of good we've done, but simply by this: that God values us highly enough to give us joy.

We live the good life out of gratitude. We live in the way of Christ, the way in which, by faith, forgiveness triumphs over revenge, hope over despair, joy over sorrow, generosity over stinginess, love over apathy.

God calls us to be watchful for the ways in which joy is breaking in around us. Christ is always coming. The clouds are always descending. Stay alert to how God draws near in the mighty injustice that grabs our attention and begs for our passion. God draws near in the spiritual awakening that puts us in touch with a heart that we had forgotten we had. God draws near in the thing of beauty that reminds us that the world is more than just its ugliness. Who knows what form it will take, this reign of God that is always drawing near us? Be watchful for it. Look for it in the midst of the routines.

Wake up to whatever your life is bringing you. Wake up to pain because we can't be healed until we admit that we're hurt. Wake up to the love we won't let ourselves feel, because we're afraid our hearts will break. Wake up to the job we've been given—watching for God's presence.

"My Life Has Never Been the Same"

Scott Gunn • March 10, 2019 • Luke 4:1–13

A friend of mine told me how she came to be transformed by an encounter with God's word. As a child, she grew up in a household that went to church, but she didn't get any exposure to an actual Bible. Visiting a friend's house—a home where the family was very involved in their Baptist church—my friend saw a Bible. She was curious, and she somehow turned to the first chapter of John's gospel.

"In the beginning was the Word, and the Word was with God, and the Word was God. . . . And the Word became flesh and lived among us, and we have seen his glory, the glory as of a father's only son, full of grace and truth" (John 1:1, 14).

It is, I think, the most beautiful chapter in the entire Bible. My friend was captivated. She copied down that poetic chapter onto a piece of paper and kept it with her for years. Through the words of scripture, the Word made flesh transformed her. Her life has never been the same.

During Lent, I encourage you to decide how you might use this season to turn to Jesus, to reject those things that draw you away from him. If you already have a plan, wonderful. But if you don't yet have a plan, perhaps you will take a suggestion. Find a Bible. Or find a Bible app or a Bible website. Every day of Lent, read a few words of scripture. Read a gospel. Read the Bible from the beginning. Read the psalms. Read the invigorating story of the early church and the Holy Spirit in the Book of Acts. Find an index and read about a topic that interests or concerns you. Whatever you do, read. Read God's word.

We do not live by bread alone. We live—we truly, fully live—when we are nourished by the bread of life and our thirst is quenched by the living water. Jesus shows us the way in all things. And today he shows us that the scriptures can be our companion when we are tempted, when we are most in need.

Our life's journey is full of challenges, full of relentless temptations. How can we resist the temptations to turn away from Jesus? How can we make sure we hear the still, small voice of God amidst a din of competing noises? We can turn to the Bible. We can open our hearts. We can bask in the glory of God's love for us as it is revealed in the scriptures.

We might find ourselves saying, "My life has never been the same."

"The Seasons of Life"

Thomas Lane Butts • April 14, 1996 • 1 Corinthians 15:50–58

Each season of life has in it certain inherent tasks that must be accomplished if we are to grow into the next, unimpeded and unimpaired. And if by circumstance or neglect we do not resolve the issues of one season of life, these unattended issues attach themselves to us and plague us from one season to the next until they are resolved in some manner.

Admittedly, there are those for whom life has been such an unhappy experience that the whole idea of eternal life of any sort seems to be more of a wicked threat than a happy promise.

But in spite of this anomaly, we want life, more life than we now see. The very nature of God suggests life after death. The justice and love of God, the nature of humankind, and the nature of life itself, the heart of the teachings of Jesus and of the whole New Testament, call us to believe in life after death.

I do not ultimately believe in life after death because of any mindboggling philosophical arguments, as convincing as they may be. Any rational arguments, taken individually or collectively, leave enough unanswered questions about life after death to seriously impair a confident approach to the grave. I believe in life after death because Jesus said, "Because I live, you shall live also" (John 14:19). I trust the word and the promise of Jesus. I do not understand the mechanics of how this will be.

My heart frames questions for which the mind has no ready answers. I do not know the way, but I trust both the person and the living direction of the one who said, "I am the way, the truth, and the life." I believe what Jesus said about life and death, and life after death, comes from God. He knows the answers to questions that I cannot answer. He not only *knows* the way, he *is* the way—and I will follow him to and through and beyond the grave.

For the Christian, belief in life after death hangs, finally, not upon any rational arguments that the mind can frame, but upon faith in the veracity of one solitary person, whom we believe to be the divine Son of God, Jesus of Nazareth, who lived and died and indeed rose from the dead, giving final substance to his most radical promise and claim.

Jesus, in his teachings, assumes the everlasting quality of life. He admits no possibility that a person may escape from life by dying. What we have become in this life, for better or worse, we take with us into a new setting, the exact nature of which we do not know or understand. When we die, we leave behind all that we have and take with us all that we are. It is a sobering thought to realize that with death we are not done with life.

"Tattooed for Life"

Debra von Fischer Samuelson • January 8, 2017 • Matthew 3:13–17

Life can hold with it joy and laughter and wonderful conversations and friendships, some close enough even to be our chosen families. And right alongside it, life can bring with it loss and disappointment and sleepless nights and an inner certainty that no matter what we do or no matter how hard we try, we're just not measuring up.

Which is why we need to tell this baptism story over and over again—to counter the story of the inner critic, to counter the story the world often tells that to be truly beloved you have to possess something: money, house, good looks, power. We tell this baptism story over and over to counter the story that we don't measure up or that we don't belong. The story of baptism is not only a story that we belong to God and are beloved by God, it is a story that we belong to each other, that we are a part of a larger story of God's presence in the world.

Several years ago the theme for Lent at my church was baptism. We wanted our people to remember their baptisms and the difference that being baptized makes in their day-to-day lives. Months earlier, in conversation with a couple of our talented artists in the congregation, the idea came up about creating a baptismal font for Lent that would somehow also be interactive. I loved the idea and they ran with it—but it ended up a little bigger than the original plan.

I was thinking of a nice little fountain with some water that would be running and maybe would splash around and draw some attention to it. But when the congregation entered the church that first Wednesday evening in Lent, they discovered a huge ten-by-ten-foot box with two-and-a-half-foot- high cement walls, with three pipes sticking up about five feet from the bottom. Around the foyer were chunks or pieces of limestone on flats, left over from landscaping jobs because they weren't the right size or the right color or the right shape for their original purpose, each one with a round hole drilled through the middle of it.

Following the worship service, the community was instructed to line up and take pieces of the limestone, pass each one down the line, and put them on the pipes until each pipe was covered to the top with limestone pieces. What people hadn't realized was that those pipes were water pipes. When they turned the water on, water started trickling out of those pipes and over the stones. And these leftover stones that had been rejected from various landscaping jobs—all different shapes and sizes and colors, now stacked together and with water sprinkling over them—became a beautiful fountain.

Those stones were *us*, we who sometimes feel rejected because we just don't measure up and yet are chosen to be part of something big and beautiful, just as God had chosen us in our baptism to be a part of God's kingdom, a member of God's family. And as we watched the water run over the stones, we could imagine God's love, shown to us in the waters of baptism, washing over our lives, bathing us in love.

We come together in worship because we need to hear over and over again that God loves us and has claimed us as beloved children, cherished and treasured. And we come together in worship because our wells sometimes have run dry and we need to feel those refreshing waters of baptism trickling over us again. Because sometimes life is just so hard that we have no words to pray or no songs to sing; we are just that empty. Sometimes it's the community of the baptized that sings those hymns we can't always sing, and sometimes it's the community that prays the prayers we can't always pray, and sometimes it's the community that speaks the words of faith that we can have trouble speaking ourselves or even believing ourselves. And we just let those words and songs and prayers wash over us, reminding us of God's love, reminding us that in the waters of baptism, God has called us and claimed us as God's own—beloved and delightful. Cherished.

That's the story of our baptisms. That's a story worth telling, over and over again. That's a story worth living in.

"Sharing in the Life of Jesus"

Juan Carlos Huertas • August 12, 2012 • John 6:35, 41–51

When we eat and drink together, we recognize that Jesus, the "bread of life," is showing us the way to one who is available and yet mysterious, showing us that we too have access to the divine life, that we too can come into God's presence.

Maybe if we spent more time and attention in becoming a "feeding people," if we put our attention in becoming a community of the "bread of life," if we took more seriously the reality of God's own presence in our meal, we would spend less time and attention on things that separate us, that exclude others, that close our doors, and that question God's image in others.

Do we gather week after week and sit in the pew and say "yes" and eat of the meal and go on with life as usual, or do we ignore it altogether as something that has nothing to do with us, as something that we might think about later at another time, ignoring the plight of those around us, continuing to push people out of the community?

Part of the challenge is to recognize that there are many around us who go each day, every day, without the sustenance needed. As we gather for feasting day after day, week after week, there are many who have no such sustenance. As we go about our political posturing and ideologies, there are many who go without. As we fight about who has worked enough, who has had enough initiative, as we argue with one another about what it takes to be "successful," as we battle as congregations across America wanting to draw the line as to who's in and who is out, we miss the point, we miss the invitation. We, like those who came back on that day, are still unsure who it is that we have encountered.

"I am the living bread," says Jesus. Open your eyes. See the light.

Maybe now we can recognize that we, too, have been beneficiaries of an amazing life. We have found our sustenance, and instead of using it to propel us into the neediness and hunger of the world, instead of having it energize us into speaking on behalf of those that have no voice, instead of having it call us to task again and again into the ways that our own life is part of the problem, we have continued eating our fill, acting as if we've earned it, ignoring the plight of those who need this sustenance the most.

The community called the church is at its core a community of people who hunger. A community of people called together around table, whose own identity is rooted in what it means to be sustained by the presence of Christ's self each and every time we gather together.

From the very beginning of the story of faith, God has been giving us of Godself, inviting us to take this sustenance and use it as a source of being the light of the world on behalf of God's kingdom. So part of our sacrifice of praise and thanksgiving is our recognition that, when we leave our gatherings of prayer and praise, we are to walk out the door and work tirelessly for the sustenance and feeding of a hungry world.

May our congregations, may our gatherings, may our conversations become the active center of creating this future, of creating eschatological reality. May we together begin to make a way to the Father in our eating. May we become a people that begin to extend life eternal, a people who live out the meaning of sharing in the life of Jesus to a hungry world.

"Life Is Gift"

John Claypool • June 13, 2004 • Luke 7:36–8:3

The insight on which Jesus built his life in ministry is in fact the loveliest truth in all the world. To put it quite simply, life is gift. Birth is windfall. None of us earned our way into this world by what we did or did not do. It was given to us out of pure generosity and out of everlasting mercy. This truth in the depth of all being is the secret of all secrets in the Christian vision of reality.

As the ancient hymn in Philippians puts it, "Jesus made himself of no reputation." And he was able to do that because he had already been given a name that was greater than anything else in the world. In other words, Jesus understood that life is given to us as a gracious gift. Our worth is not something we have to earn or to deserve, and it was this sense of life as gift that not only enabled Jesus to minister as Jesus did, but it's how he was able to open other people's eyes to the great generosity that lies at the heart of God that is, in fact, the greatest saving truth.

Jesus, at the time of his baptism, realized that he was by the grace of God the beloved child of God, and what was true of Jesus at that moment is true of every one of us as well. This is exactly what this woman and Zacchaeus had discovered and accounts for the incredible change that came over their lives.

I had a friend once who had struggled for years with feelings of inadequacy. He had tried so hard to earn a sense of worth by out-achieving and out-competing other people. But every time, he told me, it turned out to be just like cotton candy. Achievements lasted for just a moment and then turned into nothing but air in the depth of his being.

After years of seeking to earn his own salvation, one day in a hotel room he finally cried out in sheer anguish just like the Philippian jailer, "O God, what must I do, what must I do to be saved?" And he told me that to his great amazement, as he uttered his words, it was as if a hand began to write something on the wall across from his bed. And what the hand wrote was, "Nothing, nothing at all. It comes with the territory." And it dawned on him that what he had so tried to earn was, in fact, a gift freely given if he would simply accept it. He said he had what Thomas Merton calls a breakthrough to the already, an old image he had read years before came back to his mind—that of an individual riding on an ox looking for an ox. Here was somebody anxiously surveying the whole terrain to try to find something when all along what that one most wanted was right present underneath him.

This is the great truth of being saved by grace. We do not earn our worth by what we do. It was given to us by the great generosity of God at the moment of our conception. And, therefore, in this passage, it's clear to me that Jesus opened up the way for this "notorious sinner" to learn the wonder of what it means that life is gift and birth is windfall. She came that day to give thanks to the one who had opened her eyes to the deepest of all truths.

I invite you in this moment to ponder the fact that God loves you in exactly the same way that God loves every human being that God has called out of nothing into being. You already are the beloved child of God, not by virtue of what you have made of yourself, but by virtue of what God has made of you out of pure and amazing grace. I invite you, in fact, I plead with you, let God's grace be the basis of how you feel about yourself.

Questions for Meditation and Discussion

1. What does it mean to live life abundantly in today's world? Does it involve gathering material possessions around yourself? Or something else entirely?

2. In Genesis 1, God creates all life, including human life. Reading that chapter alone, reflect on the meaning of life in God's world. What is the relation in Genesis 1 of human life to other forms of life?

3. Jesus says that he has come to give life and to give it more abundantly. What does Jesus mean? In what ways is this possible?

4. Jesus is called "the bread of life." What implications does this phrase have for us, especially when we partake of the bread in the sacrament of communion?

5. Consider your baptism. How did that sacrament mark your life? Are you living according to the baptismal vows you made or were made on your behalf? Find a Book of Common Prayer and renew them (see pages 301–303).

6. Many Christians focus on their lives as a kind of station along the way to eternal life. What are the challenges and rewards of this view of life?

7. What do you think Jesus means when he declares, "I am the way, the truth, and the life"? What does he mean when he says, "I am the bread of life"?

8. **GROUP ACTIVITY:** When does life begin? As a group or in pairs or trios, find biblical passages that offer descriptions of the beginning of life, then share your findings. How do those passages describe the beginning of life? How do they describe life itself? What does living involve? How are you living your lives in these days? Do you feel that you are living life abundantly? Share your conclusions with the whole group.

2 | Faith

We claim to have faith, and it's important to us. But what do we talk about when we talk about faith? Do we think of faith as simple assent to doctrines, saying "yes" to a set of beliefs that we allow to shape our lives? Or do we see it as a response to God's revelation to us, whether in the Bible, in nature, or in Jesus? Do we distinguish faith from reason, holding those two activities in separate spheres? Or is faith simply a mystery that we can never fully define? Do we simply "know faith when we see it"? And once we declare that we live by faith, how does such a proclamation affect our actions every day? How are our faith and our morality, our ethics, our everyday life related?

Over the centuries, theologians have struggled to offer a definition of faith that illumines the depths of this relationship between a believer and God, which often seems beyond the ken of human understanding. In the early centuries of the church, councils formulated creeds so that believers could assent to doctrinal statements, thereby identifying themselves as Christians and differentiating themselves from other religious movements of the time.

For many Christians, the clearest definition of faith can be found in the familiar passage from Hebrews 11:1, 3: "Now faith is the assurance of things hoped for, the conviction of things not seen. . . . By faith we understand that the worlds were prepared by the word of God, so that what is seen was made from things that are not visible." A long list of the heroes and heroines of faith follows this affirmation of faith. The litany of the faithful, including Abraham, Moses, Gideon, Samuel, and Rahab, recalls the actions they embraced that made them faithful.

In the gospels, people are healed when they have faith in Jesus. In Mark 10:52, the blind Bartimaeus begs Jesus to have mercy and let him see again. Jesus responds simply, "Go, your faith has made you well," and Bartimaeus regains his sight. And yet there are other instances in the gospels when people are healed whether they profess faith in Jesus or not.

In the Bible, as well as in our times, doubt often accompanies faith, leading us to question God's presence, or even existence, in our lives. "Where is God?" we shout when a person dies too young. If science can explain the creation and sustenance of the universe, some people ask, why is there a need for faith in a God who creates and sustains? In an age when miracles may have ceased, many ponder, how can we believe that God interacts with others in sometimes dramatic ways? In a world where knowledge is revealed to us with a keystroke on a cell phone or laptop, why do we need to rely on faith to help us understand the world?

The *Day1* sermon excerpts in this chapter explore many of these questions, providing insight and sustenance as we consider the role of faith in our daily lives.

"Trust Jesus and Elvis"

Susan Sparks • April 11, 2010 • John 20:19–31

If only we could have the faith of Elvis fans: a faith driven not by empirical proof, but by the voice in our hearts. Finding that kind of faith can change our lives. For when you believe something in your heart, you begin to act it in your life.

Look at Elvis fans. They not only believe he lives, they *act* like he lives. For example, they are constantly looking for Elvis. The Bible says seek and ye shall find. Well, Elvis fans follow that to a tee. They are constantly looking for the *King*. And sometimes they find him. There have been Elvis sightings all over the world—from a spa in Tokyo to a

Burger King in Michigan. There was even a woman who claimed that she found the image of Elvis in a taco shell.

If only we'd put even one percent of that kind of energy toward looking for Jesus, we might actually find him, too. Maybe we'd find him in the eyes of a little child or the downcast gaze of a homeless stranger. Maybe we'd find him in the face of an enemy or the tears of a loved one with whom we are fighting. If you believe he lives, you'll act like he lives. You'll look for him and you'll find him.

Another thing: Elvis fans believe he lives, so they look for others who believe as well, like through Elvis fan clubs. I heard a story on the Graceland tour about a woman who was in a fan club called "Taking Care of Business." She had to have major surgery and afterwards received hundreds of cards and letters from "Elvis friends" all over the world. We Christians can learn something from this. Community is what gives us strength, support, and focus in times we most need it. Finding families of faith is what helps us keep our faith. If you believe he lives, you'll look for others who believe as well.

If you believe he lives, you'll act like he lives. And Jesus's message is certainly a message of action. Elvis apparently felt the same way. For Elvis said early in his career, "Music and religion are similar—because both should make you wanna move."

The gospel is a living, vibrant force that should make us want to get out and move—move around in the world, move toward each other in love and compassion, move toward bringing in the kingdom—or the blingdom—or whatever.

I want a religion that makes me want to move.

I want a savior that makes me want to put on a sequin jump suit and sing.

I want to believe in a Jesus that lives.

"The Struggle to Believe"

William L. Self • December 28, 2014 • Luke 2:22–40

Jesus was a doubter. He doubted that violence was the way, so he said, "Forgive one another." He doubted that the long prayers and rigid dietary laws were essential to faith, so he talked about a simple faith. He doubted that the Samaritans were an inferior race, so he told the parable about the Good Samaritan and a bad priest. The capacity to doubt is the prelude to faith. Strong faith always has to be fought for.

There is no such thing as a faith without tears. A generation that wishes for a faith without tears must find it difficult to adjust to the teachings of the New Testament and the facts of life. I would suggest that you doubt your doubts. Look them straight in the eye and doubt them. This takes courage but prevents them from controlling your life.

I've been a pastor for a long time and have observed that some people are growing in their faith and others are retreating. One day a church member came to my office and asked if he could have a few minutes to talk about his crisis of faith. Of course, I was glad to do it. He wanted to leave the church because he was wracked with doubts. I told him that I had to go to the hospital to make a visit and asked him to ride with me so that we could talk about it on the way. He consented, and we drove across town to a large hospital. We walked through the corridors and found the room of the patient I was to visit. The patient was a young doctor in his late thirties dying of an inoperable cancer.

As we entered the room, all the medical apparatus was hooked to his body, but he was conscious of our presence and wanted to talk. We talked for a short time about life and death. I read scripture and we prayed together. My doubting friend was there with me and stood at the foot of the bed as I stood at the patient's side. The entire process in the room took about twenty minutes. There were tears in the eyes of the patient in the bed as we turned to leave. We went down the hall to the elevator and then out to the parking deck before either one of us spoke. Finally, on the way back to the church, my doubting church member turned to me and said, "I see things differently now. Eternity has broken into my life, and I want to start over with Christ."

This is a good day to move from skepticism to faith. *Celebrate your doubts.* See them as a prelude to a deep, abiding, and mature faith.

"A Joyful Obligation"

Christopher A. Henry • October 6, 2019 • Luke 17:5–10

By the time we reach the seventeenth chapter of Luke's gospel, the disciples have been sitting at Jesus's feet for quite some time. They have been commanded to leave security behind, along with everything else they hold dear, to set out on a strange and difficult journey. They have been commanded to love their enemies, to forgive those who harm them, to give to all who beg from them. They have been urged to let go of their worries and trust God completely. And, just before our passage, Jesus commands his disciples to forgive anyone who wrongs them—even if it happens seven times a day.

In response, the disciples have an urgent plea for Jesus: "Increase our faith!" It is a reasonable request, given the context; the disciples sense that they are going to need more faith if they are to follow the teachings of Jesus.

The answer Jesus offers sounds hopeful. All you need, Jesus says, is a tiny little speck of faith, about the size of a mustard seed. That much faith unlocks whole new worlds of possibility. And implicit in Jesus's words is his conviction that the disciples already have at least that much faith. In other words, Jesus asks his disciples to trust that they have enough faith already, enough to live out the challenging commands that they have been given.

So, the disciples might be feeling pretty good about this—a little faith goes a long way and they have at least a tiny bit. But just when the disciples might be tempted to think of faith as a possession we could quantify, Jesus shifts the term from noun to verb.

Jesus asks the disciples which of them would reward a servant for working out in the field by giving them a place at the table for dinner. His question would have seemed absurd to the disciples who all lived in a culture of clearly defined functions for servant and master. Of course, a servant deserves no extra credit or displays of gratitude for doing exactly what he was required to do. The answer to Jesus's question would have been almost laughably obvious to the disciples. Invite servants to dinner just for doing their jobs? No way.

But this is a parable, so we can expect a twist. This time it comes at the very end. After telling the story in such a way that the disciples assume they are the masters, Jesus turns the table on them with these words, "So you also, when you have done all that you were ordered to do, say, 'we are worthless slaves; we have done only what we ought to have done.'" Just like that, the followers of Jesus are recast in the role of servants, due no credit or gratitude for fulfilling the tasks assigned to them. We have done what we ought to have done. It's a message about doing your duty, fulfilling your obligation, knowing your role.

Words like "duty" and "obligation" have acquired a mostly negative connotation in our culture of rights and choices. Outside of some rather small and loyal communities, it is assumed that duty is dull, a denial of our freedom to co-create the world as we would have it. If someone does something because they are obligated or required to do it, we see that as a lesser motivation. When we do good, we prefer to think of ourselves as free moral agents acting on our own selfless initiative, rather than as servants who are responding to the commands of a master or lord. We want some credit for our acts of kindness and charity; if not a banquet held in our honor, at least a place at the head table.

But the one who offers this instruction is Jesus, who came to serve, not to be served and who expects the same of those who follow him. In the church, as followers and disciples of Jesus, we are bound to fulfill our obligation. Our duty is to follow Christ's way in the world. We do not get to make up our own set of instructions and chart our own course. We are called, commanded, and compelled in very concrete ways. We don't have the luxury of hating those who hate us. We don't get to sit in the judgment seat and pronounce verdicts on those whose actions exasperate us. We are not permitted to grasp selfishly on to what we have and withhold from those in need. We are not even allowed to let anxious worry overcome us. We must do our duty. Not because we are wonderfully magnanimous people (though we may well be) but because we are servants, students, disciples, followers—called to do our part as residents of God's realm. And I would suggest that there is both freedom and joy in living this way.

"Faith, Friendship, and Fruitfulness"

L. Bevel Jones III • May 25, 2003 • John 15:9–17

The key to this scripture is that Christ has chosen us, asked that we be on his side, a member of his team. We didn't pick him. He sought us out, recruited us as it were—not by coercion, nor by conscription, but out of loving care, out of belief in us, out of concern that we get to know him, enjoy fellowship together, and become all we are capable of being.

This is the key to understanding the message of the Bible. All we are and do as people of faith is in response—get that word—in *response* to our Creator's gracious overtures and actions in our behalf. We are called, chosen, and cherished by the One who created us. What an honor and privilege!

The late Dr. Paul Sherer quickens the conscience and heightens the imagination with this insight:

> The fundamental joy of being a Christian consists not in being good. I get tired of that. But in standing with God against some darkness or some void and watching the light come. The joy of religion is in having your fling, by the mercies of God, at shaping where you are, as a potter shapes a vase, one corner of God's eternal Kingdom.

This can happen when we get it right, that is, when we catch on to Jesus's analogy of himself as the vine, you and I as the branches, and God as the vinedresser. That system works: the vine drawing its energy from the sun, the soil, and rain; you and I drawing strength from the vine; and God controlling and cultivating the whole process.

God, after all, has chosen us. God is with and in us, and God is in charge empowering us. You see, as committed Christians we are not doing our work. We're not even doing God's work. God is doing God's work through us.

That's why Jesus makes the astounding statement that the Father will give us whatever we ask in his name—not anything we want, not anything that we might try to do, but what God wants and wills to do through us. And let us never forget: The main thing is to keep the main thing the main thing, and that's the main thing. And what is the main thing? To love one another.

"Wake Up and Believe!"

Ozzie E. Smith Jr. • November 16, 2014 • 1 Thessalonians 5:1–11

At the end of the movie *School Daze*, the cast looks out at the audience and says, "Wake up!" I remember when watching that movie a gentleman behind me said, "I'm tellin' ya, 'cause I slept through the whole movie!" That remark caused me to think of what that moviegoer missed while asleep. That movie dealt with the divisive issue of light and dark skin among African American Greek organizations on a college campus.

The apostle Paul also deals with the differing hues of Christians being children of the day as opposed to skeptics of darkness. Not unlike that moviegoer who missed not only the movie but the message, we miss the message when we don't stay awake as Christians, when we don't wake up and keep the faith. One of the most powerful and amazing things about the Word of God is its power to renew and encourage us to witness—to wake up. Our witness then can become a candle on a dark and windy hill. It becomes light in the midst of darkness.

The late Rev. W. Herbert Brewster penned, "If you walk by faith and not by sight, though dark and starless be your night, Christ the bright and morning star will lead you on, and you'll never be left to walk alone." The words *dark* and *starless* and *night* are quite a contrast from the "bright and morning star" of Christ. And such is the tenor of Paul's message to the converts in Thessalonica. They had become Christians because of Paul's bold and light-bearing witness. He introduced them to Jesus Christ and he stayed at it. They, as Zora Neale Hurston once said, had been touched by the kind of love that makes your soul come out of hiding—the love of Jesus Christ.

Yet, their virgin faith was always subject to the dark counsel of resident skeptics preoccupied with Christ's second coming and other things that could not be known. Paul's preaching is a call to remember the gospel in the midst of prevailing gossip. His presence, his kind of zeal could hardly be ignored—he kept at it, refusing to be dimmed or discouraged by darkness or even death threats.

Paul keeps the Thessalonian converts focused on what they *can* know rather than what they *cannot* know. They can know that Jesus is coming, but they cannot know the Day of the Lord. They can know that knowing Jesus beats having all the answers. Many have followed leaders claiming to know about the Day of the Lord. Yet, like a thief in the night of their dark counsel, the answer escapes capture. Jesus told the disciples that such knowledge was unknown even to him. Thus, Paul reminds them who they are and should continue to be, children of the day rather than sleepers in the night. Not falling to the hype of peace-claimers or readers of the times. Wake up and keep the faith!

It is no wonder the psalmist says, "The Lord is my light and my salvation. Whom shall I fear? The Lord is the strength of my life. Of whom shall I be afraid? When evil doers assail me to devour my flesh, my adversaries and foes, they shall stumble and fall. Though an army encamp against me, my heart shall not fear. Though wars rise up against me, yet I will be confident." All because the Lord is our light.

"If you walk by faith and not by sight, though dark and starless be your night, Christ the bright and morning star will lead you on. And you'll never be left to walk alone."

"Keep the Faith"

Michael Curry • August 18, 2013 • Hebrews 10:32–11:1

Faith. The prophet Habakkuk said, "The righteous shall live by faith."

Faith. Jesus said, "If you have faith the size of a mustard seed you will say to this mountain be moved from here to there and it will obey you."

Faith. When Jesus healed folk, he told them, "Go your way, your faith has made you well."

Faith. The book of Hebrews says, "Faith is the assurance of things hoped for, the conviction of things not seen."

Faith. St. Paul said we are justified, put right with God by grace through faith in Jesus Christ.

Faith. Faith is the key to living the power of the resurrected life of Jesus in our lives. Faith is the key. So keep the faith.

That's what the Book of Hebrews is getting at, I think. The chapter begins, "Faith is the assurance of things hoped for, the conviction of things not seen." And then it goes on after sort of defining faith. It goes on to give examples of people who lived by faith. When you look at the list, these folk all shared some things in common. Every one of them swam against the current of their time. Every one of them marched to a different drummer. Every one of them lived against the odds. And each one made a difference for the kingdom of God.

My friends, faith is a gamble, but it's not a crazy gamble. It's a gamble on the God who loves us, a gamble on the God who has given us life, a gamble on the God who has shown us the way to live in love and compassion, in decency and kindness. It's a gamble that the God who created us knows how to show us how to live.

You keep the faith. Keep the faith when you feel like it, and keep it when you don't. Keep the faith. Keep the faith when you think you know what you're doing, and keep the faith when you don't. Keep the faith on the mountain top of exaltation, and keep the faith in the valley of humiliation. You keep the faith in the God who has faith in you, who has given you life because he has faith in you. And that faith will keep you.

Questions for Meditation and Discussion

1. How do you define faith? Can you find or think of other definitions of faith you've heard? How does your definition compare?

2. How is faith related to your baptism? How do we enact faith in the sacraments?

3. Why do we so often call faith a mystery? Is it solvable?

4. Think about times you have doubted your faith. What were the reasons for your doubt? In what ways has faith overcome your doubt? Has doubt made your faith stronger?

5. Who are the models of faith in your life? Your parents? Grandparents? Other family members? Friends? Why are these people your models, and how do they exemplify faith for you?

6. Why does Jesus equate healing with faith? What does that mean regarding your own healing needs?

7. Have you ever known a person who lost their faith, or simply grew cold to it? Why do you think that happened? What might people do to keep their faith strong and active?

8. **GROUP ACTIVITY:** Read Hebrews 11 together. Discuss the various ways that the individuals listed in this chapter practiced their faith and became examples of faith. Focusing on verses 1–3, reflect on the writer's definition of faith and how it might play out in your lives.

3 | Love

n his *Protestant Hour* sermon on February 1, 1976, "There Are Many Ways to Say I Love You," Presbyterian minister and beloved children's television personality Fred Rogers of *Mister Rogers' Neighborhood* said, "In this world there are many ways to say, 'I love you.' It seems to me that one of our most important tasks as parents and Christian educators is to help and encourage both children and their adults to discover their own unique ways of expressing love."

Love is indeed the essential principle of the Christian faith. Without love there is no Christianity. Even so, loving God and loving others may be the most challenging aspect of living as a disciple of Jesus Christ.

Most Christians can recite Jesus's "greatest commandment" without pausing for a breath. It's a commandment rooted in the Hebrew Bible and Jewish ethical admonitions of Jesus's time: "You shall love the Lord your God with all your heart, and with all your soul, and with all your strength, and with all your mind; and your neighbor as yourself" (Luke 10:27).

Yet, when we're called to embrace loving God and others, we often hesitate and grasp for some definitions that might help us clarify exactly what that means and how to do it. Questions echo within our hearts. What does it mean to love God with all my heart? With all my soul? With all my mind? Who is my neighbor? What does it mean to actually love them? How do I demonstrate my love for God with all my heart day by day?

Although Jesus's commandment is clear and concise, it may be the most difficult for us to embody and live out naturally. If I don't like my neighbor, how can I be expected to love them? If my neighbor acts despicably, what shape should my love for them take? In fraught political times, when countries or states or even families are divided by a tenacious antagonism that assumes all others are enemies not worthy of our love, how do we practice this commandment?

This raises the fundamental question, what is love? When people don't approve of others' behaviors, they may say, "I hate what you are doing, but I love you." Or, "I don't have to like you, but I love you." Even more confusing is a saying Christians often utter perhaps without thinking: "I love you because God loves you." Regrettably, this statement often comes across as if the person saying it feels required to love the other person merely out of obligation—"well, only because God loves you do I love you." Is that really love? Does God instead call us to surround the other with the powerful and transformative energy of love, regardless?

Meditating on questions such as these can form the basis of a lively journey to find ourselves as God's beloved who in turn loves fully and authentically.

In his *Protestant Hour* radio series on "The Four Loves," which later became a popular book, author and theologian C. S. Lewis helped to explain the different forms of love expressed in the original Greek language. For instance, when we talk about love, we may confuse familial love (*storge*) or even erotic love *(eros)* with God's love (*agape*).

To be sure, some medieval mystics such as Teresa of Avila loved God in an almost erotically charged way, with the passionate abandonment that a lover loves her beloved. Yet, Teresa abandoned herself to God in ways that most Christians cannot. What's more, in our society erotic love is often one-sided, focusing on what one person can give the other. One person may abandon herself fervently to a lover, but the other may simply receive such affection and passion passively, as a receptacle for the lover's passions. Erotic love can be selfish, focusing only on self-gratification.

We might also think of love between friends (*phileos*). While such love may seem to be deeper and more reciprocal than erotic love, it nevertheless lacks the depth and power that the love of God requires. Because love between friends draws on mutual attraction, individuals still choose the objects of their love and attention. And friends may "fall out" of friendly love, as when one breaks a promise, cheats or lies or breaks trust, or simply holds an opinion the other can't abide. Disagreement or lack of trust drives a wedge in the friendship, and the love between friends falls away.

Above all this, the love Jesus describes in his commandment (*agape*) is the most demanding love of all because it requires us to give up our desire for receiving love in return for offering our love. It requires us to go deeper, to love as Jesus loves. The kind of love that Jesus proclaims in his ethical admonition isn't at all selfish; it's selfless. It's God-centered, not me-centered. It transcends self even as it requires the self to be engaged with others in soul-changing and heart-altering actions.

In one of his *Protestant Hour* sermons, C. S. Lewis described *agape* this way:

> *Agape,* love itself, is not a hunger that needs to be filled, but a fullness that gives away. Insofar as we become capable of that sort of love, *Agape* is entering our lives. . . . *Agape*—God's love to the created—is doubly a gift. He gives us his love and with it the gift of loving. By receiving and responding to *Agape* from him, we become able to exercise *Agape* toward others.[3]

---

3 C. S. Lewis, "The Four Loves," in *The Protestant Hour: 35th Anniversary Celebration* (Atlanta: Protestant Radio & Television Center, 1980), 1, 3.

Paul reminds us in 1 Corinthians 13:13: "Faith, hope, and love abide . . . the greatest of these is love." The love of God nourishes us, and in turn we can offer others spiritual nourishment by sharing the bread of God's love with them. The *Day1* sermon excerpts in this chapter illustrate the challenges, the hope, and the power of embracing and practicing agape love.

"The King of Love"

Michael Curry • November 25, 2018 • John 18:33–37

This truth about love—love that is unselfish, sacrificial, seeking the good and the well-being of others before my own unenlightened self-interest—is particularly vivid in the Gospel of John. For John's gospel, the Crucifixion and Resurrection of Jesus from the dead was the ultimate cosmic battle between the titanic powers of sin, evil, and death, and the ultimate power of the love of God. As John sees it, there is an organic and intimate connection between the love of God, the self-sacrifice of Jesus on the cross, his resurrection from the dead, and the salvation, liberation, hope, redemption, and reconciliation released because of that.

Let me show you what I mean. At the Last Supper in John's gospel, chapters 13–17, Jesus prepares his followers for his death by teaching them about love. It is fascinating that if you look at the New Testament gospels, you will discover that Jesus speaks most consistently and profoundly about love as he is heading toward the cross. It's at the Last Supper in John's gospel that Jesus says, "I give you a new commandment, that you love one another." It's at the Last Supper that he says, "Just as I have loved you, you should also love one another." It's at the Last Supper that Jesus says, "By this everyone will know that you are my disciples, that you love one another." It's as Judas is slithering out of the room, as Peter will soon deny him, as he will soon be betrayed and handed over to selfishness that Jesus says, "As the Father has loved me, so have I loved you. Now abide in my love." It's at the Last Supper in John's gospel that he says, "Greater love has no one than this, but that they give up their life for their friends, and I have called you friends."

This way of love that Jesus teaches as he is about to give up his life is not sweet, soft, or sentimental. This way of love is the way of living that is unselfish, sacrificial, seeking the good and the welfare of others before one's own unenlightened self-interest.

That way of love is a game changer. It's a game changer in my personal life. It's a game changer in all our personal lives. But it's also a game changer in our social life, our political life, our economic life, and in the global life of the world.

Love is the key that opens up the paschal mystery of his death and resurrection.

Love is the reason and the cause for which Jesus sacrificed his life, and it is the energy and power that would soon, even after his death, quake the earth, roll back the stone from the tomb, and raise him from the dead, new and transformed and transfigured.

This love is the key to our living in the power and the dynamic energy of the risen life of Jesus.

"The Prophet Mary"

Barbara Brown Taylor • March 21, 2010 • John 12:1–8

Today we are headed to a home in the Jerusalem suburb of Bethany, where Jesus stopped in to see his old friends Mary, Martha, and Lazarus before he entered the city for the last time. He loved them, John tells us, although he does not tell us why. Maybe there is no "why" to love. They called him Lord, so they knew who he was, and yet they were not his disciples, at least not in any formal sense. They were his friends, the three people in whose presence he could be a man as well as a Messiah.

So Mary rubbed his feet with perfume so precious that its sale might have fed a poor family for a year, an act so lavish that it suggests another layer to her prophecy. There will be nothing economical about this man's death, just as there has been nothing economical about his life. In him, the extravagance of God's love is made flesh. In him, the excessiveness of God's mercy is made manifest.

This bottle will not be held back to be kept and admired. This precious substance will not be saved. It will be opened, offered, and used, at great price. It will be raised up and poured out for the life of the world, emptied to the last drop. Before that happens, Jesus will gather his friends together one last time. At another banquet, around another supper table, with most of the same people present, Jesus will strip, tie a towel around his waist, and wash his disciples' feet. Then he will give them a new commandment: Love one another, as I have loved you.

At least one of the disciples will argue with him, while others will wonder if he has lost his mind. But a few will watch him working on their feet and remember Mary bending over *his* feet like that—the prophet Mary—who knew how to respond to Jesus without being told, the one who acted out his last, new commandment before he ever said it. Remembering her may help *them* leave *him* alone while he finishes delivering *his* message.

At home in Bethany, the storm clouds are still piling up against the door when Mary gives the forecast: it will be bad, very bad, but that's no reason for Jesus's friends to lock their hearts and head to the cellar. Whatever they need, there will be enough to go around. Whatever they spend, there will be plenty left over. There is no reason to fear running out—of nard or of life either one. For where God is concerned, there is always more than we can ask or imagine—gifts from our lavish, lavish Lord.

"The Vulnerability of Love"

Laura Mendenhall • April 16, 2000 • Mark 14:1–15:47

Love involves a willingness to put oneself at risk, and God, who is love, was willing to risk great suffering, willing to risk betrayal and denial and desertion, willing to risk mocking and misunderstanding. There has been no pain greater than what God's love can bear. God does not regret the price of love. Such vulnerability is perfect love.

I want to protect Jesus from the vulnerable stance of love, for I hear Jesus praying with the psalmist,

I am the scorn of all my adversaries, a horror to my neighbors, an object of dread to my acquaintances. Those who see me in the street flee from me. I have passed out of mind like one who is dead. I have become like a broken vessel for I hear the whispering of many, terror all around as they scheme together against me, as they plot to take my life. But I trust in you, O Lord. I say, "You are my God. My times are in your hand. Deliver me from the hand of my enemies and persecutors. Let your face shine upon your servant. Save me in your steadfast love."

Jesus chose to be vulnerable. And during the events of the week following the Palm Sunday parade, those who witnessed God's love in Jesus Christ found themselves to be in a position of vulnerability as well.

The days after the parade were frightening and sad for the community of faith. As C. S. Lewis wrote, "To love is to become vulnerable, to risk suffering. If you want to make sure your heart is not broken, you must give your heart to no one, to nothing. Then, it will not be broken. Indeed, it will become unbreakable, impenetrable, irredeemable."

Those who followed Jesus in the parade became part of the vulnerability of love. They could have taken their loved ones home from the parade and shut themselves off from the events of the rest of the week in an effort to protect themselves from the vulnerability of love. Yet to do so would have meant being cheated from the reality of God's love for them, being cheated from what it means to love one another.

"What's Love Got to Do with It?"

Shari L. Rates • April 29, 2012 • 1 John 3:16–24

What's love got to do with it? Love is the impetus, the driving force in achieving the unimaginable; a closer relationship to the Creator of all things. Love is the compelling force that says, through the mercy and grace of God, we are truly capable of extending the same to one another.

What a powerful testament to that which is attainable for us all through belief. Only the love of a God who was willing to sacrifice everything for God's creation could be provisional for us to experience the same. Eighteenth-century pastor John Vianney once said, "Love for our neighbor consists of three things: to desire the greater good of everyone; to do what good we can when we can; to bear, excuse, and hide other's faults. The kind of love that Jesus is talking about here is the sacrificial love of the Cross, not the superficial love of this world."

You see, it is at the foot of the cross where we are humbled to realize that without the love of God for each of us, how would we ever be able to love others?

Therefore, may our days be blessed with opportunities to show the love of God in whatever form it presents itself to do so. And may our obstacles and barriers be removed through the power of prayer and our attentiveness to the disciplines of the faith. And in so doing, may God's mercy and grace be a sustaining force and focus as we seek to live under the auspice of a selfless and far-reaching love. God's love.

"Legacy of Love"

Ashley Rosser Wilson • May 25, 2014 • John 14:15–21

What does *love* really mean? Our society is obsessed with the notion of love. It is in our romantic comedies, showing us that in the end true love always prevails. It is in our books, which help us to reflect on the different ways we show and receive love. It is in our music, no matter the genre. We even have a holiday dedicated to celebrating love, as if it is the only day all year where showing our love counts most.

But what does the Christian faith say about love? Throughout the New Testament, we encounter many definitions and descriptions of love, some mysterious and others more evident. We know that God is love and that God loves us so much that Jesus, God's only son, was given to us.

However, we can learn more about what love means to Jesus through other parts of the legacy he left the disciples. He said to them, "I will ask the Father, and he will give you another Advocate to be with you forever" (John 14:16). Out of Jesus's love for his followers and for God's love of both Jesus and humanity, an Advocate, or helper as it is translated from Greek, would be sent to Jesus's followers.

It is also important to note that Jesus said *another* advocate. Jesus is also an Advocate sent by God to the world, to reconcile it, to love it, and to draw humanity closer to God through his life, death, and resurrection. Thus, after Jesus was no longer physically with his followers, the Spirit would walk with them and guide them in the way Jesus walked with them and guided them. The Spirit would be with the followers as Jesus was with them.

It was as if Jesus knew his followers would need assistance in living a life of love as he, the ultimate embodiment of love, did. Luckily, for them and for us, the Spirit they were given would be with them forever: the Spirit was *with* them and *within* them. The Spirit would be part of his legacy, reminding his followers of his legacy and guiding them as they strove to live into it.

So here, to love is to be an advocate, to give oneself for others as Christ gave himself for us, and as God gave of Jesus and the Spirit. This definition of love is illuminated throughout the gospels. We see Jesus loving, advocating, and in ministry with the poor and the marginalized, women, persons with disabilities, lepers, strangers, and the imprisoned. He fed the hungry and healed the sick. And the list goes on. These are all part of his legacy.

We are to continue loving our neighbor and seeing them as God sees us all, in word and in deed. This Spirit is still moving among and within us today as we continue Jesus's work of love. We too have not been left alone in the task we are called to as believers. But how are we to live into Jesus's legacy? How do we reflect, live into, and embody love?

"The Manifestation of Undefeated Love"

Nathan Baxter • April 7, 1996 • John 20:1–10

This is what Easter is about for believers: it is about God's undefeated love for us. Because of Easter resurrection we know our worst cannot destroy the love of God revealed in Jesus Christ.

Good Friday represents the worst that humanity can do. It represents our effort to destroy God's offering of love: "For God so loved the world that he gave his only begotten son, that whoever should believe in him should not perish but have everlasting life." Good Friday represents our rebellion against that gift. Quoting the *Shema*, Jesus taught, "Love God with all your heart (affections), mind (intellect), and soul (inner being)." That is as hard today as it was in the first century.

But Easter still represents the faithfulness of God's enduring and steadfast love despite the worst we can inflict. It waits until we come to the place in our lives when we realize we need the fullness of God's love. It waits until that moment when we realize that "the weight of days" is too dreadful without God; that the masters we have chosen cannot give us peace or redemption.

For to celebrate Easter is to cease the struggle against the way of God and accept the love we have so long resisted, yet so deeply needed. For as St. Paul has said, "Nothing in death or life, in the present or the future, in this world or the world to come can ever separate us from the love of God which is in Christ Jesus."

"The Problem with Two Spouses"

M. Craig Barnes • July 27, 2008 • Genesis 29:1, 10–12, 15–20

Falling in love is not a matter of the will. It is something that just happens to you. You don't choose to fall in love. But you certainly do have to make choices if you are going to stay in love after you realize that you're involved with a human being. It's pretty hard to make yourself love someone. That is especially true if it is someone who is not who you thought, someone who has disappointed you or hurt you.

The Bible calls us to love even our enemies. So the chances are good that God also expects you to truly love Leah or Jacob, or the parent who was too hurt to love you well, the friend who wasn't there for you in a time of need, or the colleague who betrayed you at work. Those relationships didn't start bad. But somewhere along the way you discovered this person is not who you thought he or she was. The people who were supposed to love you hurt you.

When we are hurt, the temptation is great to put as much distance between them and us as possible. But Jesus is persistent in calling you to return the hurt with love.

Sometimes it seems like there is no human way you are going to be able to do that. And that is exactly the right starting point. There is no human way to love this person. You will have to turn to something sacred.

If you choose to be more loving, the first place to turn is not to your strained relationship, but to your God who is love (1 John 4:8). And what do you find when you turn to God? The most amazing grace— God really knows you and God really loves you. Most of the time we think we can have one or the other—either we can be really known or loved. But if we want people to love us, then we are terrified of letting them know all the truth about us. God really knows and really loves you. That fills our hearts with so much gratitude that the love spills over into our relationships. If your heart is not filled with gratitude, even for the Leah or Jacob in your life, then you missed the miracle of the gospel.

God doesn't just love the ninety-five percent of you that is good. God loves all of you, even the five percent that seems so unlovable. That love is what transforms us and those we love. You don't get rid of your own flaws. You certainly don't get rid of someone else's flaws by trying harder. You're not asked to improve on those you love. That is up to God. We are only called to love, with devotion. That is not a love that says, "I will love you in spite of the five percent." It is a love that says, "I will love all of you and will settle for nothing less than all of you including the flaws. Otherwise the flaws will always be between us." There may be a blessing for you even in the flaws.

Once you choose to love the flawed people in your life, then you are free to choose how you will perceive these flaws. There is a strange problem in the Hebrew text when it comes to describing Leah's eyes. Our scholars are not real sure how to translate the word. Sometimes it is translated as *weak*, as to say, "Leah had weak eyes." Other times the word is translated as *lovely*, as to say, "Leah had lovely eyes."

The difference between weak and lovely is significant, but clearly it can be interpreted either way from the text. The Bible translators have to make a choice when they come to this strange word. Will they translate as *weak* or *lovely*? It could be translated either way. Leah's eyes could also be translated either way by Jacob when he looked at her. He chose to see them as weak, but he could have chosen to see them as lovely.

When you look into the eyes of your loved one, long after you have discovered who this really is, what do you see, the weakness or the love? Well, that is your choice.

"Loving as Jesus Loved"

John Claypool • May 9, 2004 • John 13:31–35

Let us never forget we're made in the image of extraordinary love. And doing what Jesus did in loving each one he ever met as if there were none other in all the world is at least an ideal toward which we can reach even if it always remains utterly beyond our complete grasp.

Need love, C. S. Lewis says, is always born of emptiness. It is basically inquisitive to the core. A need lover sees in every beloved object or person a value that he or she covets to possess. Need love moves out greedily to grasp and to appropriate for itself. If one were to diagram it, need love is always circular, reaching out to the beloved to transfer value back to itself. In a popular image, need love sucks essence out of another and into itself. It does not take exceptional imagination, Lewis contends, to acknowledge that many times when we humans say to another, "I love you," what we are really meaning is, "I need you, I want you. You have a value that I very much desire to make my own, no matter what the consequence may be to you."

Now over against this graphic image, Lewis contends there is another reality that is utterly different. It is what he calls *gift love*. Instead of being born of emptiness or lack, this form of loving is born of fullness. The goal of gift love is to enrich and enhance the beloved rather than to extract value. Gift love is like an arc, not a circle. It moves out to bless and to increase, rather than to acquire or to diminish. Gift love is more like a bountiful artesian well that continues to overflow than a vacuum or a black hole.

Lewis concludes this contrast by saying that the uniqueness of the biblical vision of reality is that God's love is gift love, not need love. And then he says, "We humans are made in the image of such everlasting and unconditional love." Lewis's depiction of gift love really is the foundation stone of the way St. Augustine describes the way Jesus loved. And the great good news for every one of us to hear today is not only that we are loved by God in this marvelous way, but also that this is our deepest identity as well and is a way we can choose to live our lives.

You and I, with the help of God's unfailing grace, can grow into the wonder of loving each one as if there is none other in all the world to love, and loving all as we love each.

Questions for Meditation and Discussion

1. In his sermon, John Claypool draws on C. S. Lewis's distinction between "need love" and "gift love." Is this distinction helpful to you? Can you describe a recent situation where you have acted according to "need love"? What about a situation where you have acted with "gift love"? Consider the emotional response you had to each.

2. Have you ever regretted the price of love, or the sacrifice you have made for love? Can you name a time when you gave up everything for love, or when you performed an action in the name of love, without seeking any praise or reward for your actions?

3. What are the fears, concerns, misunderstandings, or personality traits that prevent you from being a fully loving person, from loving as Jesus loved?

4. Ashley Rosser Wilson says that "to love is to be an advocate." What does being an advocate mean to you? How are you an advocate for others? How is your love shaped by your advocacy?

5. Who are your enemies? What do you call them instead of "enemies"? Make a list of them. Do you love them as Jesus loved? What is preventing you from loving them? Pray for your enemies. Are there obstacles preventing you from doing so? If so, what are they, and what steps might you take to overcome those obstacles?

6. Describe a situation where you had to practice "tough love." How did you demonstrate God's love for the person, or persons, in need of God's love?

7. Read Luke 10:25–28 and reflect on it. Who is your neighbor? How do you define the word "neighbor" in today's world? Can you love your neighbor? Do you love your neighbor? What prevents you from doing so?

8. **GROUP ACTIVITY:** Divide into smaller groups. Each group will come up with its own definition of love. What are the characteristics of love? How does erotic love differ from God's love? Name a few places where you have seen God's love at work in recent days. How has God's love been at work in your life? Where have you seen God's love at work in your life? Can you share God's love with others by telling those stories about seeing God's love in your life?

4 | Grace

I n 1972, the late soul singer Aretha Franklin released what is perhaps her finest album, *Amazing Grace*. Recorded live at the New Temple Missionary Baptist Church in Los Angeles, Aretha's album revealed the depth of her gospel roots, having grown up singing in church. The centerpiece of the album is the old gospel standard "Amazing Grace." Aretha's version is unlike any other: she stretches out the first note of the song over several measures, allowing members of the congregation to enter the song at the place where the Spirit moves them.

"Amazing Grace" is such a familiar gospel song that we sometimes sing it without hearing the lyrics fully and deeply. To receive grace involves an admission of our shortcomings, acknowledging that we have treated others as less than God intends us to treat them, acknowledging that we need God's love, God's forgiveness, and God's redeeming power. Can we hear the words of "Amazing Grace" anew when we live in a culture that often looks for easy answers and cheap grace, in a society that seldom acknowledges human shortcomings? Would it ever be possible to hear the words of this familiar hymn in a fresh way?

In a world that is too often characterized by judgment and law, the sweet strains of grace are too often difficult to hear. In a world where people too quickly judge one another's actions, where people too often act in ways that marginalize others, where people too hastily condemn rather than forgive, and where people are blind to the love revealed in the beauty of God's creation, it is often a challenge to see grace in action or to perceive its amazing character to restore broken relationships and heal the world.

Grace indeed turns our world upside down. Like the prodigal son embraced by his father in Luke 15:11–32, we can be surprised by acts of grace that reverse our expectations. We often expect to be judged for our actions, but we are just as often startled to receive the gift of grace from others or from God. Grace shatters our expectations.

In his ministry, Jesus exemplifies grace, loving the unloved and those cast aside by their society. He becomes our model for acting with grace toward others and the world at large. When we demonstrate grace to others, we act with the righteousness and mercy of God. When we act with grace, others see God in us. As God acts graciously toward us, as Christians we then act graciously toward others, with love and mercy and forgiveness.

Still, grace does not come easy. It's easier to judge than to act with God's grace toward others. The *Day1* sermon excerpts in this chapter nourish us with feasts of grace, asking us to ponder the challenges and rewards of acting with grace.

"Finding God in Unexpected Places"

Victoria Lawson • November 24, 2019 • Luke 23:33–43

Grace is in the ability to forgive. What exactly does Jesus mean, "Father, forgive them"? Is he aware of what is happening? He has been falsely accused, unjustly tried, and is looking in the face of death, yet his concern is for the ignorance of those responsible for his death.

Forgiveness is a central theme in the gospels. Jesus himself forgave sins. He also emphasized that God's forgiveness is conditioned by the believer's willingness to forgive others. We see the beauty in grace as we see our own stories in the faces of those that seem to be the least of our concerns in forgiving. We are able to forgive when we understand that the image of God within us and others is never destroyed by what we have done, are doing, or will do. The beauty in such a response from the

Savior is truly unmatched. Grace is always in Jesus's response to us, and it's almost always unexpected.

There is something in us all that seeks comprehension in even the most incomprehensible situations. Although we know that we have been forgiven and given grace so freely of our Savior, there is still a part of us that attempts to somehow reimburse him. But that's the thing about grace, it keeps no receipts.

Yes, it is unlikely, unruly, and often unexplainable. It's pure, seemingly simple, and untainted by our desire for control. It is not based on or biased by our perceived track record of righteousness. It is a deliberate choice to see our faults and yet continually provide all that we need. Grace is forgiveness. Grace is the ability to come before the throne freely with our concerns. It is given as a lock without a key, because grace doesn't change its mind. Never held over our heads as a constant reminder of how unworthy we are, rather the posture that drives our gratitude.

It is as precious as a choice ruby, yet to be passed along selflessly. It is sufficient. Beautiful. Paid in full and experienced at the cross by one who was once a stranger, now seated at God's table. Grace—unexpected grace—is a portrait of Jesus the Christ found in the strangest of predicaments. Receive it wholly, give it fully, and you too will begin to notice it in the most unlikely places.

"Which Comes First: Grace or Repentance?"

Robert Dunham • March 14, 2010 • Luke 15:11–32

Perhaps no scripture text has logged more pulpit time in our culture than the parable of the Prodigal Son. It is a storehouse of sin and redemption, of grace and the refusal of grace, and one can read it from several different perspectives—the father, the prodigal, the older brother. Over the years, preachers have tried all sorts of approaches to unpack its riches. I read once of one who gave a sixteen-week sermon series on the parable; after the sixteenth sermon a woman greeted the pastor at the door of the church and said, "I'm so sorry that poor boy ever ran away from home."

I know this story still packs the power to shock and offend, because it speaks of grace, and grace not only has the *power* to offend us today but *does* offend when it is exercised. What many people still want, I think— today as much as ever—is some assurance that their right behavior and right belief count for something. The notion of unmerited grace still bothers many of us a great deal.

Several years back I preached a sermon on this text, one that spoke of the embrace of sinners, whether the sin was profligate living or prideful self-righteousness. At the door several people said all the talk about grace made them uncomfortable, that grace could be made cheap when not linked to repentance. One man told me candidly that he was ready for me to stop preaching about grace and start preaching about repentance. After all, he said, repentance is always the precursor of grace.

I don't know exactly what prompted me to say what I said in response, but as I recall I made an uncharacteristically categorical statement. "There is not a single instance in the gospels," I said, rather assertively (wondering even in the moment if I were right), "when Jesus requires repentance before he extends grace or healing or hospitality. Not one. Repentance is a *response* to God's grace, not a prerequisite for it. Grace always comes first."

"Grace Upon Love"

Karoline Lewis • April 7, 2009 • John 12:1–8

What does love smell like?

Mary's love for Jesus is a rather smelly event, much like grace upon grace should. A dab on the neck won't do when it comes to matching the love Jesus has for us.

Mary's act is an act of abundant love—and it's all in the details.

The house was filled with the fragrance. There's nowhere you can go without smelling it. It seeps into your clothing, even into your skin, and the perfume costs three hundred denarii—almost a year's salary.

One denarius was a day's wage. In today's currency that eight dollars an hour, eight hours a day, for three hundred days is $19,200. So, we're talking $20,000 worth of precious perfume poured out on Jesus's feet.

This is grace upon grace kind of love. This is abundant love. The kind of love that has to be shown, not just said.

And Jesus's gratitude and love will then be the same for his disciples. Because in the very next chapter, he washes his disciples' feet, showing them the kind of love that Mary showed him. This is what happens when abundant love is let loose. This is what happens when you experience a kind of love, an amount of love, that you could never have imagined. You cannot *not* do the same.

The kind of love to which we are called, dear friends, is a no-holds-barred love. An overflowing, unending, kind of love. An abundant love.

Discipleship love is grace-upon-grace love. Love that can't stop at sufficient or succinct. Love that can't stop at "that's enough" or that has an end in sight. Love that can't stop at the level of love the world is willing to deem acceptable.

We are called to a grace-upon-grace love that lays down one's life for one's friends. A grace-upon-grace love expressed in nothing less than the taste of the best wine. The smell of the bread of life. Seeing for the very first time the world God created for us. Hearing your name called when no one else seems to care. A grace-upon-grace love expressed in nothing less than the feeling of the gentle touch of one you love.

"Grace"

Douglas Oldenburg • October 27, 1996 • Matthew 2:1–10

Grace. We read of it in scripture, we sing of it in church, we hear the word in sermons, but what is it? Perhaps most of us would respond that the closest synonym for the word *grace* is the word *love*. And we are right, of course, but there is a danger here, for *love* is a very slippery word today and can mean a variety of things.

You see, the word *grace* is needed because it refers to a special, specific, distinctive kind of love: the love of God revealed in Jesus Christ. In the

Christian community, there is a sense in which we can never talk about grace in the abstract, for grace, in the Christian context, is very specific; it is the grace of our Lord Jesus Christ. It is defined by *who* he is, or better, by *what* he does. He is the one who transforms grace from an idea, an abstract concept, into a reality. He embodies it, he incarnates it. He defines it.

Yes, you may discover it reading the Bible—many Christians have. But you might find it first reading something else, and later find its fullness in the Bible.

You may discover grace in your prayers—many Christians do. But you might discover it also talking to a friend.

You may discover it in church around the Lord's Table in a broken piece of bread and a cup of wine—many Christians have found it there. But you may also discover it drinking a cup of tea or coffee with someone at a kitchen table Monday evening.

You may encounter it in your church—I trust you do. But you may discover it in a sense of wonder as you walk through the beauty of God's creation.

You may discover it, or it may discover you, when your heart is bursting with joy. But you might encounter it when your heart is heavy with sorrow or despair or self-disgust.

Yes, it's focused in Jesus Christ, but still it's all around us; we're surrounded by it. So look for it, listen for it, and sometimes when you least expect it, it is as though a voice were saying "yes" to your life. "You are loved, you are affirmed, you are set free." Accept it, embrace it, trust in it, let it penetrate every fiber of your being, and let it make a difference in every aspect of your life.

"Amazing Grace"

Bob Bohl • March 16, 1997 • Mark 14:32, 15:39

Some months back, following a funeral where we sang the hymn "Amazing Grace," someone asked me if I would write a sermon on that "amazing grace." I have been collecting thoughts for months but confess to you at this moment I feel a little like St. Augustine, who when asked "What is grace?" responded, "I knew until you asked me, but now when you ask me, I do not know."

So what is this thing called grace? I dare to speak to some degree for both of us when I say neither you nor I can come up with clear, precise definition of grace. Maybe that is because grace is something we experience but cannot always define.

In the course of life, I have seen hundreds of examples of God's grace being experienced. People talk about what they are experiencing, about what the church has meant to them at a particular moment of joy or crisis. Some new sense of God through a Bible verse or a prayer, some new feeling of satisfaction that came from doing something for others—delivering meals, helping with a Habitat house. Some new glimpse of what God is really like at the birth of a child, a baptism, a wedding, and even seeing the goodness of God at the time of the death of someone we love—a goodness that tells us we can trust God to care eternally for them. Some new understanding of God when we find ourselves helpless on our own to handle life, and the moment we admit it God comes to our rescue.

There is a phrase we use frequently that can be misunderstood. I hear people say, "There but for the grace of God go I." If by that we mean God's grace is selective and only a few are recipients of God's grace, then we make God into something of a monster. But if we say that God's grace is free, unmerited, unearned, undeserved, but must be received before it becomes real, then and only then can we say, "There but for the grace of God go I." Not in condemnation of others but in pity for them that they refuse God's grace, God's goodness to them. But if we say, "There but for the grace of God go I" and do nothing for those who have not welcomed God's grace, then we are guilty of trying to hoard God's grace selfishly for ourselves.

To live by God's grace means that we learn to take nothing for granted, but to take whatever comes with profound gratitude to God, knowing that God will be with us to inspire us and to empower us—no matter what comes, and no matter what happens.

"The Transformative Power of Grace"

Susan Crowell • August 27, 2017 • Romans 12:1–8

This reshaping and restructuring that Christ is doing in our lives requires humility. And humility is a real challenge for all of us. We are an arrogant, self-focused people. We want what we want when we want it. We can become so focused on our own wants and desires that we become blind to the needs, opinions, and concerns of others. In our pompousness, we begin to believe that the goodness and blessing in our lives is a result of who we are, a testament to our power and ability.

Humility requires the dawning recognition that we are all completely reliant on the power of God at work in our lives. On our own we can do nothing, but with the power of Christ at work in our lives we can do all things. All of it, every good deed, every act of kindness, every gracious word spoken with gentleness—all of it is a testament to the power of God at work in and through us.

Through compassion and humility, God is transforming our lives. When grace becomes the structuring reality in our lives, transformation occurs. We begin to see that all people have value and worth. We begin to recognize that God has gifted all people with unique gifts and abilities, special ways to support and build up God's kingdom. We come to understand that all gifts are equally important in the kingdom—the gift of teaching, the gift of preaching, the gift of washing dishes, the gift of washing people, the gift of compassion, the gift of cheerfulness, the gift of tithing. All gifts are equally valued in the eyes of God.

When grace becomes the structuring reality in our lives, we begin to see the value and worth in every human being. We see ourselves as no better or no worse than any other person. We come to understand that as God's beloved, precious baptized children, we are all loved, honored, valued, and celebrated.

God is at work transforming our lives so that we might transform the world. Look at your own life. Consider the places where you are struggling. Think about the people who are difficult for you, the ones who have hurt you, the ones with whom you disagree, the ones who see the world so differently from you. How can you extend grace to that person? How can you infuse a word of grace into that situation? How can you model the grace of God for the world?

God is reshaping and restructuring our lives around God's grace so that we can reshape and restructure the world around God's grace. God is transforming us for the sake of the world. It is up to us—people of faith—to enable the world to see and understand the value of every human being. God loves, honors, values, and celebrates all of humanity. This includes marginalized populations—the mentally ill, immigrants, the LGBTQIA community, the poor, the hungry, the homeless. This includes people of other faiths—Jews, Hindus, Muslims, and Buddhists. God loves, honors, values, and celebrates all of humanity. Our calling is to help the world see the value in every human being and to strive for peace and justice for every human being around the globe.

"Down by the Poolside"

Homer Henderson • May 16, 2004 • John 5:1–9

Now who is this person down by the poolside? Who is this thirty-eight-year-old crippled castoff of society? Most of the time when we hear this story, read the story—I'll admit, preach on this story—we celebrate him and romanticize the man's combination of genuine faith in Jesus and intestinal fortitude to pull himself up by his own bootstraps. After all, didn't he believe Jesus and so was healed? Didn't he obey Jesus when he got up, picked up his mat, and walked around? This is the kind of person who really deserves to be healed. One who decided to "trust and obey, to be happy in Jesus, because there's no other way." You see, he played by the rules of both faith and practice—down by the poolside.

Jesus healed this man not because of who he was, but because of who Jesus was. Fred Craddock talks about this story as a parable of God's grace, the undeserved and unmerited love of God. That's a radical idea, and it's right at the heart of the gospel of Jesus Christ. It's the reason Jesus taught. It's the reason Jesus could teach, "Love your enemies and pray for those who persecute you," not because of who they are, but because of who you are as my disciples.

We talk a lot about the grace of God in church, that God loves us because of who God is, not because of who we are. We say God even loves us in spite of who we are. And yet, when we talk about helping others, loving others as God has loved us, reaching out to those on the margins of our society, doing something about poverty, we're really talking about helping the "deserving poor," those we call the "truly needy."

So we pass laws that make it more and more difficult for those down by the poolside. We make it more difficult for them to qualify for public assistance and health care. We pass laws that make it more difficult for children who don't speak our language to get an education. We support laws that perpetuate the status of gay and lesbian persons as second-class citizens, and so on and so on. The bottom line as a nation and often as churches, we heal not because of who we are but because of who they are, not because we're called to be healers and instruments of God's grace as disciples of Jesus Christ, but because, and only if, they deserve to be healed.

By the way, I am asking—not telling—you what this story from John asks me. Does all this talk about the grace of God have anything to do with how we live our lives, how we vote, how we decide our politics, or even how we perceive ourselves to be the church of Jesus Christ?

I don't know how it is with you, but I'm grateful every day that God deals with me according to who God is, not according to who I am. I don't have any trouble at all singing the hymn, "Amazing grace, how sweet the sound that saved a wretch like me."

"Shackles That Won't Shrink"

Gary Manning • October 25, 2009 • Romans 6:12–23

Through God's unmitigated, unmerited, and unrelenting grace, we have been set free from the power of sin. This is not a grace that merely assuages our guilt. This is not a grace that simply enables us to feel better about ourselves. This is not a grace that only attends to some ethereal part of us we call our "soul." By no means.

This is a grace that pursues us with God's love. This is a grace that pummels us with God's mercy. This is a grace that prosecutes us before the bar of God's judgment and declares us righteous. This is a grace that parts the floodwaters of sin and opens for us the way that leads to a new way of being—the way of God's life, the way of eternal life.

Grace breaks the shackles of sin and secures us in the shackles of God's righteousness. We are no longer free to do as sin pleases. Instead, we are bound irrevocably to God. Paul exclaims, "Thanks be to God that you, having once been slaves of sin, have become obedient from the heart . . . having been set free from sin, [you] have become slaves of righteousness."

Bound to God, we are engaged in the mission of God in the world. And the mission of God is not merely to rescue people's souls from some sort of eternal perdition. God's mission begins now. God's mission is here. God's mission is the healing of the world, the wholeness of humanity and the renewal of creation. We all get to join that mission, because we have been conscripted by God's grace.

When the goal is "happy harmony," every statement is vetted for its potential social or political impact. Can't say this, it might offend the Republicans. Can't say that, it might offend the Democrats. Can't say this, it might offend the Hawks. Can't say that, it might offend the Doves. Can't say this, it might offend theological conservatives. Can't say that, it might offend theological liberals. My friend said to me, "After we've made sure that we haven't said anything offensive, we're left with something so innocuous there's nothing left to energize the church for mission." Agreed.

Fellow followers of Jesus, we have been captured by grace and bound to God's righteousness. What will be our response? Will we engage the mission of God? Will we work for justice, freedom, and peace? Will we be instruments of righteousness? Will we proclaim by word and example the Good News of God in Christ? Will we embody the qualities of life that are eternal?

Or—will we settle for the incredible shrinking gospel of personal piety and turn a blind eye to the poor, the friendless, and the needy in our own neighborhood? Will we ignore the suffering of millions of children who die for the lack of clean water and fifty cents' worth of antibiotics? Will we remain silent about the futility and cruelty of war and war's inability to capture fear and slay insecurity? Will we capitulate to the power of sin that pays off in death?

Since we are shackled to God's righteousness, do we really have a choice?

Questions for Meditation and Discussion

1. What does grace mean to you? If you're having trouble formulating a definition, why do you think that might be?

2. Think about the ways you have learned personally about grace. What church teachings about grace have had the greatest impact on you? Have these sermon excerpts helped you better understand grace?

3. Reflect on your favorite biblical passages about grace, whether cited in this chapter or not. What do these passages teach you about the power of God's grace and our role in being agents of God's grace in the world?

4. Listen to Aretha Franklin's version, or another favorite version, of "Amazing Grace." How does this gospel song speak to you today?

5. When was the last time you engaged in an act of grace toward someone else?

6. What do you think are the obstacles and challenges to your living a life filled with grace?

7. How are grace and forgiveness related? How are grace and repentance related?

8. **GROUP ACTIVITY:** Discuss the parable of the prodigal son (Luke 15:11–32). Focus the discussion on each character in the story one by one. Does the younger son deserve his father's grace? Is the older brother right in protesting against his father's actions? With which character in the story do you most identify?

5 | Forgiveness

Ouch. Remember that time a friend, family member, or colleague did something that hurt you deeply? More than one time, no doubt. Whether it's a partner breaking the trust of a sacred vow, a friend lying about an act they've committed, or a family member's betrayal for monetary gain—in those moments it can feel as if the wound created can never be healed. At first we might think we'll never forget the act and the painful feelings associated with it, declaring that we're never, ever going to forgive that person. Can the damage ever be undone? Will the scars ever heal? Can we ever look at that person, let alone love that person, again?

And above our personal relationships, we must also consider the role of forgiveness in our society at large. If someone commits a crime against us or our family or friends—whether it's a felony or misdemeanor, a heinous crime or one that violates our sense of security—how are we supposed to react? Such acts are hard to forget; they shape our memories and actions for years to come.

When the person who committed the crime is arrested and brought to trial, should we rejoice that they will no longer be able to commit such crimes and advocate locking them up for life? If they are sentenced to death, are we joyful that their life will now be taken, just as they took our loved one's life? Or, can we ever forgive this person who violated us? Could we stand in the courtroom and say to them, "I forgive you"? Would uttering those words from our hearts and souls free us from the burden of living with their actions the rest of our lives? Would it even be possible to befriend this person, and in large or small ways support them, so that they, experiencing our genuine forgiveness, might have a change of heart about others?

There's a scene toward the end of the movie *Almost Famous* in which a mother's prodigal children return home. Mother Elaine and daughter Anita fight over Anita's longing for freedom, over Elaine's attempts to control her daughter by dictating the music she can play in the house and the friends she can have. After the argument, Anita leaves home with her boyfriend to become a flight attendant, becoming estranged from her mother. Anita's younger brother, William, also leaves home, but with his mother's tentative blessing. Elaine struggles with these separations, but at the end of the movie the children return home—William gladly, Anita reluctantly. As Elaine and Anita look at each other, uncertain what to do, Elaine suddenly hugs her daughter and declares, "I forgive you." In that moment, the unity of the family is restored, and the movie ends with the family sitting down to the breakfast table, laughing and telling stories.

While this movie makes forgiveness look easy, we all know how difficult the act of forgiving someone can be. And yet, this easy forgiveness in *Almost Famous* can remind us of Jesus's parable of the prodigal son (Luke 15:11–32). In that story, the younger son turns his back on his father and brother and runs off to squander his inheritance in a city where he knows nobody and no one knows him. He wastes his money rapidly and wakes up to realize what he's left behind. Upon returning home, he asks his father to forgive him—acknowledging that "I am no longer worthy to be called your son" (Luke 15:21). But his father simply, suddenly directs his servants to prepare a sumptuous meal to celebrate his return. Although the older brother protests such lavish treatment of his foolish brother, the father fervently rejoices, for this younger son had been lost to him and is now found—the torn relationship made whole again.

This story, too, can make forgiveness look easier than it often is. In two other passages of the gospels, Jesus demonstrates the difficulty of forgiving others, while at the same time illustrating ways that forgiveness is found at the heart of the Christian faith.

In Matthew 18:21–35, Peter approaches Jesus and asks, "Lord, if another member of the church sins against me, how often should I forgive? As many as seven times?" Jesus replies, "Not seven times, but, I tell you, seventy-seven times." Here, "seventy-seven" is an intensifier that means, in effect, there should be no limit to forgiveness. Jesus is pointing to the dynamic, ongoing character of forgiveness: we don't stop forgiving those who have hurt us or broken our trust in a single act; rather we continue to forgive them as we move through our relationships with them.

And earlier, as part of the Sermon on the Mount, just after he taught his disciples the Lord's Prayer, Jesus ties human actions with divine activity as a way of reminding them how powerful acts of forgiveness are. In Matthew 6:14–15 Jesus says, "For if you forgive others of their trespasses, your heavenly Father will also forgive you; but if you do not forgive others, neither will your Father forgive your trespasses." Jesus is illustrating that forgiveness is not simply a human act, but is an act that grows out of a dynamic and ever-evolving relationship with God.

Finally, Jesus himself provides a model of forgiveness. As Jesus is led to his crucifixion with two other criminals, he utters the words that reveal the ultimate act of forgiveness: "Father, forgive them; for they do not know what they are doing" (Luke 23:34). Even at the point of death at the hands of those falsely accusing him of crimes, Jesus has the compassionate presence of mind to pray that God will forgive those attacking him.

In the *Day1* sermon excerpts in this chapter, various preachers offer nourishing insights into the complexities of forgiveness as well as guidance on forgiving others and, sometimes, ourselves.

"The Freeing of Forgiveness"

Robert M. Zanicky • October 7, 2001 • Matthew 18:21–35

Forgiveness is not passive resignation to a bad situation. Rather, forgiveness is to be a positive, joyful activity in which we change from seeing ourselves as victims to seeing ourselves as victors. Forgiveness enables us to move from weakness to strength, from inadequacy to self-affirmation. The presence of the divine in our lives is perceived in forgiving others.

Forgiveness is so nuanced. We need to forgive. We need to repent, apologize, change our ways. We need to clear the air. We need to forgive in order to be forgiven. We also need to forgive for purely personal reasons. As you know, people can be cruel. Yes, you've heard it from this "neo-Calvinist." There are those who will never repent, ask forgiveness, and they will glory in your pain. There are times when you need to let go of all that heartbreak and forgive the past. Now, if you don't like the word *forgive* for this, use another word—*let go, break free*—but allow yourself to be free from the past hurt and pain that has gone on without reconciliation. It takes two to reconcile. It takes one to forgive.

You are not excusing the action. You are not ignoring the wrong, the sin committed, and the person responsible. You are not eclipsing justice. What you are doing is setting yourself free from the weight of harm that you have carried far too long.

Over the years I've seen too many wonderful people, children of God, dragged down into despair over what another has done to them. With no chance for reconciliation, they just kept hold of the anger and harm, not knowing what to do with it, ever reliving the pain, allowing the perpetrator—long gone—to hold them in their power.

Forgive. Let it go. Release it. Throw it out. Take back the God-given power you have for your own life. For some, the time is right. For others, it will take time and healing. Perhaps you need to talk with someone. But take control.

Forgiveness is not weakness. It is not passive, not gutless. Forgiveness and being forgiven are part of the fabric of being human. Serious issues stare us in the face when we consider forgiveness. Forgiveness is healthful. Forgiveness is freeing. It may take time. It may be one-sided. But it will release you. It will set you free.

"Forgiving from Your Heart"

Alex Evans • September 14, 2014 • Matthew 18:21–35

Here is the deal: most of us accept the premise that forgiveness is supremely important to Jesus, that Christians should forgive. What we struggle with is how to practice it.

How do we move from where we often find ourselves—hurt, angry, victimized, abused, alienated—to where we can say, "I am more than that. God calls me to more than that"? How do we get our minds and hearts from thoughts of anger and hurt and revenge to sincere forgiveness from our hearts? That is what Jesus wants from us.

There are two tools that Jesus uses to motivate us here. First is grateful response. God forgives so much; we are called to forgive. Goodness intends to lead to goodness. Grace intends to evoke gratitude and then more grace from us. But it does not always happen like that, so there is another motivator: punishment. When the slave fails to respond to generous forgiveness, there is the threat of torture: "So my Father will also do to every one of you, if you do not forgive."

Which motivator most speaks to you? Some of us are motivated by positive news that calls forth our very best toward the kingdom of God. In Jesus's story, we have been given immense grace just like the slave of the king. Then some of us seem to be motivated by fear and punishment.

Look, forgiveness is so central to life, and if we like the idea but fail to implement forgiveness into our heart and life as disciples—well, we are promised torture and suffering. Jesus wants to motivate us to faithful lives as disciples—lives that actually practice forgiveness, not sometimes, not seven times, but always and endlessly. What Jesus wants is "forgiveness from our hearts." Not ideas like, "Well, I can forgive, but I cannot forget." That is not forgiveness from your heart. Or we say, "I know I am supposed to love him, but that does not mean I have to like him." That's not forgiveness from your heart.

To forgive does not mean we condone what was done to us. To forgive does not mean we acquiesce or deny justice. To forgive means to refuse to let what happened destroy us and alienate us from God and from one another. It demands hard work and vigilance, but it is the way to life and discipleship and to God.

"The Justice of Forgiveness"

Kathlyn James • July 13, 1997 • Matthew 18:21–22

The thought dawns: what if forgiveness isn't primarily for the sake of the person who commits an injury? Granted, forgiveness might release that person to die in peace, or to begin life again and do things differently than they did before. But they may also be unavailable or unrepentant. So set aside the well-being of the injurer for the moment. What about the one who has been injured?

Think for a moment of a time when you were betrayed. Doesn't the memory revive the old pain, make it hurt again? Suppose you never forgive—you feel the pain each time your memory lights on the person who did you wrong. In that case you are being controlled by the pain of your past. It is impairing your ability to love and trust and be at peace in the present. Who is being hurt now by your lack of forgiveness? What could be more unfair to you than the wretched justice of not forgiving?

Forgiveness is something we must do, not for the sake of those who have hurt us, but for the sake of our own healing.

Why does Jesus command us to forgive the people who hurt us seventy times seven? Because forgiveness is something even better than fairness. It is the way we are set free.

"Unforgiven"

Alex Joyner • September 15, 1996 • Matthew 18:21–35

Benita was quiet for a long time. She looked down at the counter and flicked away a crumb left by a previous customer. Finally she looked at her sister again. "Sunshine, I don't know whether having a face-to-face meeting with mercy is going to change Dad or not. Probably not. There's too much pain there—the pain of losing his son—the pain of feeling like a failure at life.

"But I do know that sometimes it's not so much being forgiven as learning how to forgive that changes people and makes them realize that God is there. It's not easy. And it doesn't mean we go around saying 'let bygones be bygones' or that we gloss over the pain. God knows I've done my share of screaming and yelling because of Dad. And I'm not there yet.

"Forgiveness isn't something you can do all at once and then mark it down on some 'been there, done that' list, Sis. It's a process. And it takes time. And I've changed a lot more than Dad has. But you know what? It's worth it."

Jesus said, "Not seven times—not seventy times seven—but from your heart you must forgive." And it's not easy. It's a process that takes some time. But the consequences of remaining unforgiving or unforgiven are too great to bear. In a world of pain, forgiveness is a gift. Thanks be to God.

"An Exhortation to Forgiveness"

Courtney Cowart • September 11, 2011 • Matthew 18:21–35

If September 11, 2001 was the day we came face to face with the horror of a morality of vengeance, so was it also the day that those of us who were there and later served in the recovery began to learn how real the astounding beauty of unlimited mercy and love really is.

For many of us the witness to its power is embodied in the first responders and the recovery workers who served tirelessly on their hands and knees for nearly a year inside the pile to reclaim the remains of every life lost. Days after the attacks, thousands upon thousands of strangers, recovery workers, and volunteers came together in a little church called St. Paul's Chapel and formed an alliance that practiced the extraordinarily demanding spirituality of forgiveness 24/7 for nine months. In the chapel these practices poured out of us with an intensity and passion that actually surpassed the intensity of hate, even as enormous as hate's smoldering presence and sickening stench still was. As real and vivid as the horror of vengeance, so became for us the truth Jesus teaches in our lesson today. Unlimited acts of mercy free us all.

Safety, dignity, our precious web of relationships—all those human necessities that violence and trauma destroy—regenerated in this chapel, in this fellowship, so rapidly and to such an extraordinary degree that being in the sanctuary was likened to touching the face of God. The thickness of the loving energy was a force field that hit you physically when you entered. By the grace of God, these blessings we desperately needed multiplied through the practice of one thing: thousands upon thousands of acts of mercy. The chapel's atmosphere worked on us, formed us, healed us, and eventually, as its reputation spread throughout the world, drew many of the great survivors of trauma whose devastating experience made them peacemakers for life.

Most moving for me was a day in the springtime of the recovery when a delegation of survivors from Hiroshima and Nagasaki, the original Ground Zero, came to St. Paul's as guests of Colleen Kelley and the 9/11 Families for Peaceful Tomorrows. There they stood in an American church, having traveled across the world to say to us how sorry they were for our losses. In their message of condolence, they offered to us the healing balm that absolves and forgives, renewing their own humanity and making us all one once more:

> What you have done here is the perfect expression
> of the spirit of Hiroshima and Nagasaki, where so
> many survivors renounced revenge forever. Instead

they worked ceaselessly against violence and for the world as a whole.

And I hear the prayer of dismissal prayed at the national service of mourning at the Washington National Cathedral immediately after the attacks:

Go forth into the world in peace. Be of good courage. Hold fast to that which is good. Render to no one evil for evil. Strengthen the fainthearted. Support the weak. Help the afflicted. Honor everyone. Love and serve the Lord.

Perhaps this is a prayer we can hold in our hearts as we sift our lives to find the part of the world that is within our reach to mend with acts of kindness, forgiveness, and mercy. For as Jesus said, it is an accumulation of acts—seven times seventy—an unlimited number of acts, repeated without ceasing by those who will not give up, that creates a future distinct from the past, that incarnates the kingdom of God.

"The Superhuman Act"

Thomas Lane Butts • September 6, 1998 • Matthew 6:8–15 and 1 John 1:8–10

Forgiveness is a superhuman act. It requires a source of strength that we do not have on our own. Some offenses are easily forgiven. Others we can put into perspective, and we may get away with nothing more than a slight scar; but there are some offenses and hurts for which forgiveness is humanly impossible. This message is not just for neurotic grievance collectors, in whose life littleness expresses itself in many unlovely ways. It is also to those who have experienced some Mt. Everest offense that threatens to overshadow all of life. It is to those who labor under an offense that is larger than life—too big to carry and too serious to turn loose. In your mind you know that keeping it will not resolve the problem. But you are so glued to it that giving it up will require a superhuman act. It is an emotional tar pit.

Forgiveness must become for us as much a lifestyle as grievance collecting tends to become a lifestyle for the unforgiving. Once is not enough. How we all hope and pray that we can conquer evil in our lives in one decisive battle, but as desirable as this goal may be, it is not a very realistic hope. The way of forgiveness is not one decisive battle. It is a running fight. We will constantly be confronted by occasions in which we must forgive and forgive again.

It is not easy to forgive an offense that we do not understand, but in the greater scheme of things it becomes necessary if we are to have peace in our soul. It is also necessary for us to find some way to forgive ourselves, for we are the most frequent offender against ourselves. If you cannot forgive yourself, even as God has already forgiven you, then you are caught in a double bind. You are the sinner and the one sinned against.

"The Day God Ran"

William E. Flippin Jr. • March 10, 2013 • Luke 15:1–3, 11–24

In the far country, the prodigal learned the meaning of misery, but back home he discovered the meaning of mercy. Every confession a Christian makes bears witness to this, because every confession, public or private, specific or general, is made and given subsequent to the one baptism we receive for the forgiveness of sins. We are forgiven in baptism not only for the sins committed before baptism, but for a whole lifetime of sins yet to come.

Our challenge is to be like that father—our God, who ran and opened his arms to the lost, those who are bullied, those who are discriminated against for their sexual orientation, those who are seekers and even doubters of the faith. It is the mission of the church to open its doors to all the lost souls in this life.

In fact, just opening the doors is not enough. The God who runs to meet our needs teaches us that we must be willing to race out to the sidewalk, into the neighborhoods, and up to closed doors, proclaiming the promise of forgiveness and extending embraces of welcome and acceptance. Like the waiting father in this week's parable, the church, filled with Christ's love and Christ's joy, just can't sit still and wait for the slow, hesitant approach of lost ones. Like that prodigal son's father, it is our mission, our mandate to "jump with joy" at the sight of the lost stragglers journeying slowly in our direction. And to help them get the picture that, in Christ, their failure isn't final or fatal.

"Excuses, Excuses, Excuses"

Martin Copenhaver • July 31, 2011 • Genesis 3:1–13

I am going to make a bold statement here: excuses have no place in the Christian life. As Christians, we don't have to make excuses. We may still offer excuses, to be sure, but we don't need to. In fact, it is something like a lack of faith to offer excuses. We don't need to offer self-justifying excuses. In fact, we can't justify ourselves. That is God's job. After all, we are, in Paul's wonderful phrase, "justified by grace through faith." There is another way to put it: We are free to recognize that we are not perfect people. We can do that because we rely on the perfect love of God. So the Christian alternatives to excuses are confession and forgiveness.

I don't know how it is with you, but sometimes I am tempted to throw some excuses in with my confessions. "God, here's what I did and I'm really sorry, but let me tell you why I did that. I had my reasons. Everyone has their reasons."[4]

But that's not really a confession, is it? Author Kimberly Johnson advises, "Never ruin an apology with an excuse." That's good advice that applies to confession as well: never ruin a confession with an excuse. We can afford to do that because we rely on the forgiveness of God.

How big is that drawer where God keeps our excuse notes? It's got to be really big. But it is not as big as God's capacity for forgiveness.

---

4 Or, as United Methodist minister James W. Moore put it in his *Protestant Hour* series, which became the title of his popular 1998 book, "*Yes, Lord, I Have Sinned: But I Have Several Excellent Excuses.*"

The other alternative to making excuses is to practice forgiveness with one another. What if we regularly offered one another assurances and signs of forgiveness? And what if we were in faith communities that regularly, consistently offered forgiveness to one another? Would we need excuses anymore? That is, after all, the kind of life that we are called to live. We are regularly to forgive one another in the name of the God who continually, consistently forgives us all. And if we do, there is no longer a need for excuses.

We expect that in the world it will be excuses, excuses, excuses. And sometimes it will be that way with us as well. After all, such habits are hard to break. But what if we really believed in the forgiveness of God and could rely on the forgiveness of one another? What if, instead of excuses, excuses, excuses, we heard forgiveness, forgiveness, forgiveness?

Questions for Meditation and Discussion

1. Can you recall the last time you forgave someone for an act? How did you feel? How difficult or easy was it to forgive the person?

2. Is it truly possible to "forgive and forget"? Should we forget?

3. What is the relationship between forgiveness and justice? How does your act of forgiveness reflect God's mercy?

4. How can we make forgiveness a lifestyle? Does it ever get easier to forgive?

5. What if the act of forgiving is not just for the person who injured us? How does, or how can, forgiveness promote healing for ourselves or others in our lives?

6. Forgiveness is supposed to be a joyful activity. Describe the ways that forgiving others has brought you joy, or the ways that it might bring joy to others.

7. How does your gratitude for God's forgiveness motivate you to forgive others?

8. **GROUP ACTIVITY:** Divide into four small groups to discuss the following biblical passages: Luke 15:11–32, Matthew 18:21–35, Luke 23:34, and Matthew 6:14–15. What are the differences and similarities in each passage's approach to forgiveness? How are they connected? Does one passage speak more powerfully than any of the others? Once the small groups have discussed their passages, discuss these in the larger group. Which of these passages speaks most to society today?

6 | Discipleship

The Gospel of Mark opens briskly with Jesus inviting people to follow him. After his baptism by John, Jesus runs along the shore of the Sea of Galilee and, seeing Simon and Andrew casting a net, calls out to them, "Follow me and I will make you fish for people."

This scene launches a gospel that focuses on discipleship: the requirements for following Jesus, the obtuseness of his followers, the disciples' wavering over his identity. Jesus's teachings on discipleship culminate in his familiar admonitions to his followers about what will be required of them when they choose to follow him. "If any want to become my followers, let them deny themselves and take up their cross and follow me. For those who want to save their life will lose it, and those who lose their life for my sake, and for the sake of the gospel, will save it" (Mark 8:34–35).

Discipleship is demanding. As sermon excerpts in this section reveal, to follow Jesus we must give up our comfortable relationship with society and be ready to speak prophetic words and perform sacrificial deeds of love, justice, and service that challenge the status quo. True followers of Jesus cannot make an easy accommodation with their society, because Jesus certainly didn't with his. Jesus challenged the social structures of his time, and he requires his followers to do the same, even when following in Jesus's steps might lead to their deaths.

The gospels depict Jesus touching, healing, teaching, socializing, and eating with those whom his society had marginalized or rejected. He moved among the poor and the outcast, and his followers looked up to him as the one who was going to turn their world upside down and challenge the political and religious status quo of his time. Jesus's disciples aren't simply required to tell others about Jesus's life and teachings, they are also required to embody his love in order to help turn their own world upside down.

In his book *The Cost of Discipleship,* the German theologian Dietrich Bonhoeffer, whose tenacious discipleship led to his death, pointed out the difference between cheap grace and costly grace. The former slips into an accommodating relationship with culture, never questioning political leadership even when that leadership commits evil acts. Costly grace hews closely to the teachings of Jesus, to embracing Jesus's exhortation in Mark to take up his cross and follow him.

Discipleship takes many forms. True followers of Jesus are so deeply committed that they want to share their life in Jesus with others, encouraging others to follow Jesus, too. So disciples preach, witness, and share the good news of Jesus with others through their work in soup kitchens and homeless shelters and after-school programs, among an infinite number of other ways.

Discipleship requires embracing Jesus's final message to his own followers: "Go therefore and make disciples of all nations, baptizing them in the name of the Father and of the Son and of the Holy Spirit, and teaching them to obey everything that I have commanded to you" (Matthew 28:19–20).

The *Day1* preachers in this chapter explore both the challenges and rewards of being disciples of Jesus. They offer sustenance for the life of disciples like you today.

"Your Prophetic Voice"

Christopher Girata • February 21, 2016 • Luke 13:31–35

Small shifts in behavior, small tweaks in our habits, can create big ripples in our lifestyles. For most of us, prophetic living is not the strongest habit in their lives. Sure, going to church, being a part of a Christian community, sounds good; but taking that identity out into the world, being a prophet in the other spheres of our lives, is not a habit for us—but I think it could be.

Just imagine all the people in your life who have no connection to you and your faith community. Friends, coworkers, neighbors—there are so many people who connect with us on a regular basis who have nothing to do with our spiritual life. How many of those people live day-to-day, working hard, staying busy, just putting one foot in front of the other, but always hoping for something more? Honestly, how many of *us* live day-to-day, working hard, staying busy, but always hoping for more?

God wants so much more for us, so much more than just the daily grind. God wants us to claim our purpose beyond ourselves, to show love in tangible, meaningful ways. And when our lives bear witness to the grace of God, we become prophets to those around us.

Let me be clear with you: a prophetic life is not an easy life. We live in a world where people often choose to support destructive behavior, where too often cynicism is celebrated and hopefulness is derided. The status quo raises up and rewards self-centeredness while compassion is seen as weak. Our broken world needs prophets, and God has sent you and me to make a change. We are being called to bear witness to the radical truth of Christ, a truth that is as prophetic and vital and threatening and hopeful today as it was two thousand years ago.

You have a prophetic voice to share with the world. Whether you have a generous heart, willing to give your last dollar to someone who needs it more than you do, or you have the courage to influence your neighbors in positive, hopeful ways, you have a prophetic voice—and God is calling you to make your voice heard. No act of love is too small. No witness of hope is too small.

"The Cost and Joy of Discipleship"

J. Bennett Guess • March 16, 2003 • Mark 8:31–38

What if Jesus knows something that we don't? What if it's possible to bear the cross and discover joy at the same time? What if the two don't have to be mutually exclusive? What if by some stroke of providential irony those who lose their life for Jesus's sake will actually know an abiding joy that surpasses any temporal happiness this world has to offer?

Maybe Jesus was right and his yoke really is easy and his burden really is light, and in bearing the cross we will find not hardship but sweet rest for our souls. I mean, I wonder if Mother Teresa laughed more than the rest of us. Have you ever thought about that? I wonder if Nelson Mandela slept better than the rest of us. What if Clarence Jordan's life was actually better than your life or my life, however we prefer to define the meaning of better? I wonder about stuff like that sometimes. Because Jesus may just be correct, and those of us who are running around trying to make our easy lives even more comfortable actually may be losing out on something way more essential and much more important.

My friend, what the church needs most urgently today is not more people or more money or more programs or more ministries. We certainly don't need more buildings. But what the church needs today more than anything else is *courage*. We simply need more courage. By and large, we are afraid to risk and, moreover, we are afraid of those who ask us to risk.

Most of us have yet to move beyond the sweet and sentimental aspects of our faith to begin to discover the real hard stuff that Jesus asks of us, to wrestle with the realities of people's lives, to talk about the real stuff that matters to folk, even if it makes us squirm in the pew to have to hear it and squirm in the pulpit to have to say it. This may offend you, but I believe it is true. A great number of pastors are more afraid of their congregations than they are worried about the painful realities of injustice and, likewise, too many of us are guilty of counting the cost before we consider the worth. As my mother says, "We would rather *seem* than *be*."

In a culture that seeks above all to soothe and protect while people everywhere are woefully overstressed and overworked and overmedicated, I think the cross that Jesus offers may actually be lighter than the other stuff we've been trying to carry instead. Maybe the radical way of Jesus has some advantages over the other roads we've been on.

"Practice What You Preach"

Kris Lewis-Theerman • October 30, 2011 • Matthew 23:1–12

Discipleship has nothing to do with standing out, with being self-serving, or putting ourselves first. Quite the contrary: we, all of us, are called not to be served but to serve others. Jesus consistently reminded his followers that "the greatest among you will be your servant" and "all who exalt themselves will be humbled, and all who humble themselves will be exalted."

So we're caught between what the gospel calls us to and what our culture upholds, and that's where we often find ourselves in the same bind the Pharisees were ensnared in, the bind my mother understood so well when she demanded, "Don't do as I do, do as I say." We believe one thing, we hold it in our hearts, yet our behavior all too often gives lie to that belief.

If you think I am being too hard on you, on all of us who call ourselves Christians, think about what our lives as average churchgoers are like. We go to church on a Sunday morning and we hear the good news of the gospel; we're so moved by the sermon and the hymns that we put a few extra dollars in the plate for outreach, and we vow to drop off some food for the local food pantry. We feel refreshed by our worship, and a bit self-satisfied if we're completely honest because, look, we've been to church. We say a prayer as we leave that we might be better disciples. And then we walk out of church, and nine times out of ten we leave our discipleship behind.

We don't leave it behind on purpose, of course. It's just that it's hard for us to connect Jesus saying "Love your neighbor as yourself" with the news of the undocumented immigrants who were picked up while harvesting our crops or with the homeless man sitting on the street hoping to get enough change for a hamburger at McDonalds. It's hard to connect Jesus's command to "turn the other cheek" with Congressional requests for more defense spending and reports of violence around the world. It's hard to heed Jesus's injunction not to "worry about what you shall eat or what you shall drink or what you shall wear" when the economy is going south quickly. It's hard to live up to our ideals; as Paul succinctly put it in his letter to the Romans, we do those things we hate and we fail to do those things we want to do. We don't practice what we preach.

There's only one answer to this dilemma, one antidote for what ails us. And that answer is God's grace.

God's grace for us means that no matter how many times we walk out of church leaving our discipleship behind us, God will give us yet another opportunity to live more fully into it. No matter how often we act in self-serving ways, we will be given more chances to serve others. No matter how badly we fail to live out our discipleship, to practice what we preach, God's love and God's grace are still there for us, still hold us and comfort us and sustain us.

We will always have yet one more chance—one more chance to get it right, to embrace Jesus's call to be servants, to see our neighbors at every turn, to see them and to love them, unselfishly, unreservedly. That's what Jesus teaches over and over again—and Jesus never fails to practice what he preaches.

"The Joy of Struggle"

Margaret Neill • November 15, 1998 • Malachi 3:13–4:2a,
Psalm 98:2, 2 Thessalonians 3:6–13, and Luke 21:5–19

Disciples are to be prophets in preaching the Good News of the reign of God. That preaching is not only from those persons who may stand in some pulpit at some time, or stand up in front of some group of people and proclaim on a given day, this is the Word of the Lord. But that prophetic preaching is also in the everyday lives of all of us who proclaim Christ as Lord and Savior.

This is the tough expectation of covenant relationship with God. It is that hardness that I continue to find in the Christ of Luke who sets his face toward Jerusalem and never turns back. And his teachings become more intense and more challenging for all who would hear, inviting us to do the service of God in the world. He ensures that we are gifted by the Spirit, that we will be enabled to do the ministry.

Being a disciple may have some spiritual benefits, but the economic costs seem more than most of us are willing to pay. Discipleship is high and costly work. It means paying attention, acting in the moment, persisting in spite of the hardship, and letting go of our need for glory. And then even in these lessons we are promised that the end of time is not a wonderful thing. In Malachi, for example, the day is coming, burning like an oven when all the evildoers will be stubble. But there is the promise for those who revere God's name: the Son of Righteousness shall rise with healing in its wings.

And then, Jesus says in Luke, the day will come when not one stone will be left upon another, all will be thrown down. This will give you an opportunity to testify. For I will give you words and a wisdom that none of your opponents will be able to withstand or contradict. This terrible day sounds like the future ending of all things, but could it be? Might it be our future begins? Could it not be that this right relationship with God, this struggle and hard work has a gift hidden in it as we persist to the end? And the gift is the very presence of God.

So perhaps our struggle has not been in vain. Perhaps our reflection will show us that something wonderful has begun to happen in our lives today. Because we realize that the cost of salvation is MYSELF in large and capital letters, and the gift in that cost is Christ's very self in us.

The cost of discipleship, we are told over and over, is obedience to God and, embedded in that cost, the gift of freedom. We know that the cost of work is service to us, long hours, tired bodies, weary minds. And it is all for the glory of God. And the gift embedded in that strenuous activity is joy in the Lord. The good news is that we are all followers, not pioneers, and God holds us all close throughout all our life's journey. We are indeed beloved and blest.

"Christ and Everything Else Thrown In"

Peter W. Marty • September 17, 2006 • Mark 8:27–38

Following Jesus asks for a life that in one way or another has the cross deeply embedded in it. There is sacrifice expected. We give up our lives. Playing it safe no longer is an acceptable philosophy. Death stops being a reality to be feared.

Check this out: the first half of Mark's gospel is all about "how to live." Jesus gives instructions of one kind or another on how we might best fashion our lives. And then, at this pivotal point right in the center of Mark's gospel account, Jesus makes a shift. He begins to show us "how to die." Now that we have been given a life, he demonstrates how to give it up—or how to give it away. This is a huge move.

I don't know about you, but I have found in my own life that sometimes I am more comfortable talking about Jesus than expressing some wild and passionate devotion to him. I think I'm holding nothing back, and then I realize that caring about Jesus with the insight of my mind or through the books on my shelf is not the same as giving over the full allegiance of my life. It's a little bit like the difference between talking about a loved one and actually picking up the phone and telling a person you really love them.

Maybe you recall the first time you ever told someone for whom you had strong feelings that you really loved them. Your mouth got dry and your palms turned sweaty as you sought the courage to utter those words that are so powerful: "I love you." It's one thing to acknowledge that these three words are true. It's altogether something else to speak them and to realize how powerfully true they are. Because once they're spoken, you can no longer avoid the implications of them for your life.

Something like this happens when we hear Jesus ask, not, "Who do people say that I am?" but, "Who do *you* say that I am?" The minute we hear this question rattling around in our heads, we have a choice. Either we can hold back and talk about this Christ figure whose sayings and deeds are written down in a precious ancient book, or we can decide to open up the fullness of our lives by using the language of love.

If you should choose the second option for living your life in Christ, be prepared for a wild ride. Yes, there will be some hard times and some enormous suffering, I imagine. But you will also have an incredibly abundant life, complete not only with Christ, but with everything else thrown in.

"Good News?"

William H. Willimon • October 18, 2009 • Mark 10:35–45

LOOKING FOR PEACE IN LIFE? WORRIED ABOUT THE FUTURE? Those are the questions the billboard asks. Underneath the questions, the answer: JESUS CHRIST IS THE ANSWER.

Now from what I see, this is the predominate presentation of Christianity these days: you have some need, perhaps a need for peace in a troubled life, the need for greater hope and confidence in the future. Well, Jesus is the answer.

Our scripture is from Mark's gospel, the earliest of the gospels, I assume. Mark certainly wants to reach people with the message of Christ. Mark's gospel begins with "Here is the good news of Jesus Christ." Here in Mark is the good news about Jesus.

Remarkably, when compared with the way we talk about Jesus, Mark has little to say about our felt needs, our struggles, and our difficulties. Mark mainly talks just about Jesus. And when he talks about Jesus, it's not Jesus as the answer to our problems that Mark stresses, but rather Jesus as strange and demanding Lord.

Take today's scripture. As the disciples walk along with Jesus, a couple of the disciples say, "Lord, grant us to sit at your right and your left when you come into your kingdom." Those who sit next to the chief are those who share power with the chief. In other words, "Lord, when we get you elected Messiah and your Kingdom is come, grant us to sit on your Cabinet." It is an understandable request for the disciples to make of Jesus. After all, here are the ones who have left everything and they've come to follow Jesus, to walk with Jesus along his way. Why did they commit to Jesus? Well, unlike a lot of people, they believe that Jesus was the long-awaited Messiah, the great leader who would come in, raise an army, kick the Romans out of Judea, and set up Israel again as the most powerful nation in the world.

Two disciples ask to sit next to Jesus in his glory, one on his right, one on his left. When Jesus came into his "glory," it was not on a throne. It was on a cross, with two thieves, one on his right and one on his left.

This is the message that contemporary followers of Jesus have been reluctant to proclaim to the world, perhaps because we're reluctant to hear this message ourselves. Jesus is not a technique for getting what we want out of God; Jesus is God's way of getting what God wants out of us.

God wants a world—a world redeemed, restored to God. And the way God gets that is with ordinary people like us who are willing to walk like Jesus, talk like Jesus, yes, and even, if need be, to suffer like Jesus.

"Up Ahead"

Robert C. Wright • July 7, 2019 • Luke 10:1–11, 16–20

Jesus wants to speak to his friends about the harvest. "The harvest is great," he says. He's talking about connecting with people. Sharing purpose with people. Gathering people. Some call this church growth, but it is so, so much more. More like joining God in God's purpose. More like helping people become themselves.

Harvest is God's purpose for God's people in the world. Harvest is how God's people can embody and make contemporary the phrase, "For God so loved the world . . . ." Engaging and inspiring people is the job. Gathering and collecting people in the world is what Jesus asks of each of us today.

Harvest is how God says, "Come along side me and know me." Harvest is how God says, "Join me. Befriend me. Do my will. Delight in my word." Harvest is the work God needs partners for. Not because God couldn't do it all by Godself, but because God has decided to include us in the joy of making an eternal difference in the world.

Harvest is how Jesus says to his friends, "This is an urgent matter, please focus." Harvest is what God wants us to pray for, when we are gathered together and in our own personal devotions. If the church depended on your prayers for growth, on your prayers for harvest, where would she be?

The church is harvest made for harvest. You and I have been gathered—think back—by family, by friends, into the privilege of baptism for the privilege to extend baptism. The church was not breathed into existence to tend itself; the church was made for increasing God's harvest.

First and foremost, the harvest laborer is sent by God in partnership with people of faith. He or she goes in joyful obedience and bold humility as an ambassador to comfort and confront. As God's latest incarnation in a world of hurt and beauty, for them worship is not what they do on Sunday. It is who they have become Monday through Saturday.

The laborer of Jesus's heart's desire delights to tell the story of God's love with all its consolation and its challenge seven days a week. He or she will have a remarkable ability to unfold the scriptures and declare the mighty acts of God in their own voice and in their own way. Delighted, not dire.

The laborer will mobilize people based on the mighty acts of God. Formed by God's word, those stories of old, the laborer will rescue Jesus from the church and give him back to the people. They will increase Jesus's celebrity among the sinful as a fellow sinner, and as one knowing the gift of forgiveness of their own sins.

Certainly, the harvest laborer's imagination will belong to God. The true laborer has seen God do infinitely more than they can ask or imagine, and so they are inspired to trust. They trust that God, as the still point of the circle, is drawing the circle of the harvest wider and wider and wider, and they want to join God in this work.

What I am saying is that the laborer is not a sedentary sage; their work is to search for God's children in the wilderness of this world's temptations and to guide them through its confusions, that they may come to know that life with Christ is life abundant. Remember, Jesus never actually said *wait and welcome*; Jesus said *go and make*.

This is the labor Jesus longs to see more of among his friends. This is the labor that can know a plentiful harvest.

"The One-Talent Man"

Edmond Steimle • January 23, 1955 • Matthew 25:21

The Bible always did say that unbelief is the greatest of sins. And the greatest obstacle to faith is not whether God is personal or not; not whether God is a God of love or not; not whether Jesus of Nazareth is really a divine or only a good man. These questions are not the crucial ones. This is the crucial question—the obstacle: to believe that all heaven is tremendously concerned about you and what kind of person you are.

For you see, God's biggest problem is not the big, important people. For one thing, there are only a very few of them, really, and a surprising number of them are aware of their God-given opportunities just because they hold positions heavy with responsibility. No, God's biggest problem is the likes of you and me because of this devilish—I use the word quite literally—this devilish notion that what we are and what we do is of very little moment except to a very small circle of relatives and friends. Whereas God has big plans, as God counts the word *big*, for you. And you sit there and say you don't believe it?

Do you begin to see why our Lord chose the one-talent man and put him under the spotlight? And why he was so hard on him? Because that man is you. And God wants you to know, whether you believe it or not and no matter how incredible it may seem to you, that all heaven is at this very moment wondering about you and what kind of person you are going to be. Because the only kind of heaven God knows for this earth is the heaven God can bring to the earth only through you.

Questions for Meditation and Discussion

1. What does it mean to be a disciple of Jesus? How would you define the word? Look it up and trace its root meanings. Does that change your understanding?

2. In today's world, what does it mean to "take up your cross and follow Jesus"? What is "your cross"? Remember, it's not about you—so what is it about?

3. What are the spiritual benefits of discipleship? How might they play out in your life?

4. What are some of the ways you struggle with following Jesus?

5. What are the joys of discipleship? In specific ways, how have you experienced them?

6. Who were your models of discipleship? What did you learn from them?

7. As disciples, how do we practice what we preach in our everyday lives?

8. **GROUP ACTIVITY:** Read Mark 8:34–35 together. Discuss as a group or in small teams what are the requirements of discipleship? What does it mean to follow Jesus? Name some examples of individuals you think are following Jesus in the way that Jesus depicts here in Mark. Share your thoughts together.

7 | Prayer

Prayer is fundamental to a thriving, fulfilling spiritual life. And yet it can be a challenging, even frustrating discipline for many of us. Even though the Bible is filled with examples of men and women of God praying, even though the Book of Common Prayer and other resources are filled with prayers—for guidance, for deliverance, for comfort, for confession, for family and friends, for healing, for justice—we can still feel awkward in the act of praying.

How do we pray? What should we say? How should we say it? Should we set aside a specific time during the day or night to pray, or can we pray anywhere and anytime? How long should our prayers last? How do we actually talk to God? For what and whom should we pray? Can we pray for our own healing? Does God really hear our prayers? What happens when we feel like God doesn't answer our prayers? How do we pray in public? How do we cultivate an attitude of prayer? What models of prayer should we emulate? Is it appropriate to use prayers from a book of prayers or from a prayer manual rather than using our own words?

Praying raises so many questions, but sometimes we make it far too difficult. Truly, God is creative, open to any approach we might make for holy conversation. God yearns to commune with us in prayer.

Prayer is both an intimate personal act and a corporate act that draws together the church community. Liturgical traditions include various corporate prayers as part of every Sunday morning service. Some churches hold weekly prayer services devoted to intercessory prayers for those suffering from illness or those grieving. Such corporate prayers bind the community in spiritual unity, allowing members of the congregation to raise their voices to God together for healing or guidance. Individual members are encouraged to pray privately for others in need of prayer or for themselves. Even so, what kind of power does prayer have in our lives, and how do we know that prayer works?

The Bible offers a wealth of guidance about prayer, even providing a model that we can use as a guide or repeat daily if we are unsure how to find our own words to pray. Jesus reassures his disciples that God will hear their prayers. "So I tell you, whatever you ask for in prayer, believe that you have received it, and it will be yours" (Mark 11:24). Of course, this passage doesn't guarantee that when we pray for a new job, a million dollars, or a parking space, our supplication will be granted. Notice that the passage connects faith and prayer and focuses on the attitude with which we pray: "believe" and "receive."

Waiting for answers to our prayers can test our faith. But when we embrace our faith, we understand that uttering certain requests in prayer does not mean that they will be granted, quickly or ever. What's more, the answers to our prayers may not come in the ways we expect. Praying requires our attention to details of our lives as we search for the guidance or healing that God provides in answer to our prayers.

As some *Day1* preachers in this chapter point out, Jesus offers his disciples a model, a how-to manual, for prayer in Luke 11:2–4. We call it the Lord's Prayer but it may more appropriately be called the "disciples' prayer." It includes confession, praise, supplication, forgiveness, intercession, and justice. Each verse provides a starting point for our own prayers and illustrates the depth with which Jesus understands our human condition and the ways he counsels us to begin our life of prayer.

The sermon excerpts in this chapter explore several aspects of prayer, offering wholesome and sustaining slices of the bread that feeds us individually and as communities.

"Unleashing the Power of Prayer"

Larry Goodpaster • October 16, 2016 • Luke 18:1–8

For those of us who read scriptures, who pay attention to the spiritual disciplines, who strive to be formed in our faith, we know that prayer is essential. We remember the encouragement from the apostle Paul that we should "pray without ceasing" (1 Thess. 5:17) and that we should "pray in the Spirit . . . and always persevere in supplication" (Eph. 6:18). The widow in this story in Luke 18 captures that with her tenacity and determination. But when prayers go unanswered, or we do not get what we had hoped for, a weariness settles in. We begin to give up. So what can we take from this parable that might help us unleash the power of prayer for living faithfully?

Prayer is not about bringing God a "to do" list of things we want, believing that somehow if we ask in faith and perhaps even have someone agree with us, it will be done. God does not hand out gifts based on what we want. However, prayer is about positioning ourselves to receive what God offers, confident that God will act.

One of the frustrating realities we all come face to face with at some point in our lives is the apparent delay in receiving answers to our prayers. That, however, is no excuse for giving up. Continually coming to God provides an opportunity for us to refine our prayers, or for God's grace to refine us, so that the shape and the direction of our prayers are bent toward the way of Christ and not merely in a self-centered way. We keep knocking and asking and seeking. Julian of Norwich puts it this way: prayer "is yearning, beseeching, and beholding" until we see God face to face.

It is finally all a matter of faith, of trust and reliance on God, of believing God. The widow received justice and mercy, and I suspect she was never the same again. And then Jesus connects the dots between persistent prayer and faithful living as a way of urging us to align our lives with that holy love and compassion. It is important for our spiritual lives to be engaged in persistent prayer, but it is also important to live faithfully as a result of having been the recipients of God's love, mercy, and grace.

Prayer is an act of trust that reorders our priorities and helps us to see and to live into a different future. In a world filled with fear, prejudice, hatred, and violence, we need to be living faithfully, boldly, tenaciously as people of faith who pray and strive for God's Kingdom to come on earth as it is in heaven. As we do, we will discover that we have unleashed the power of prayer to make a difference in our lives and to help shape a different world.

"We Do Not Know How to Pray"

Joe Evans • July 27, 2014 • Romans 8:26–39

Our youngest daughter is three, and when she prays she holds her hands together lining up her fingers just right and closes her eyes as tightly as she can, because prayer is a serious business; it has to be done correctly. Some people are so deliberate about prayer that I've heard them pray in King James English—a very different form of speech compared to the rhythm and inflections that they use to order chili dogs, assuming that prayer demands some kind of special effort. However, despite such efforts, despite much practice, the apostle Paul says that we do not know how to pray as we ought.

We think we should, however. We think we should know how to pray and we're scared to admit that we don't—so families invite the preacher and her family over for dinner, and while the youngest in the family usually says the prayer, "God is great, God is good, let us thank him for our food," when the preacher is around, Dad defers: "Reverend, would you be so kind as to bless our meal?" Prayer is best reserved for the professionals, it would seem.

There is a story about Jim Morrison, the lead singer for the Doors, a rock and roll band that pushed the limits of what was acceptable with their controversial lyrics and scandalous stage persona during the 1960s. The story goes that Morrison was brought to a place, the Factory, to meet the artist Andy Warhol, who greeted Morrison like the returning prodigal son, though it's not clear that they've ever met. Warhol gave Morrison a golden telephone, held it out to him, and said,

"Somebody gave me this telephone, I think it was Edie. And she said I could talk to God with it, but uh . . . I don't have anything to say. So here . . . (giving Jim the phone) this is for you. Now you can talk to God."

This is easier to believe—that it takes something magical, something special, that it must take our most formal speech and our most lofty thoughts to be heard by God, not always realizing that God is ever more ready to hear than we are to speak. Not believing that if God is for us, surely no one could be against us. Not daring to trust in the assurance that in all things we are more than conquerors considering the one who has loved us beyond measure. After all, our world doesn't work that way.

We pray that God will do what we want, praying as though we were dictating our will to our attorney: give this to him and that to her and don't let that one have a thing. But we do not know how to pray as we ought.

Should not prayer be the act of giving up on our will and trusting in God's? Should not our prayer be the relinquishing of our limited power while placing all our hope in God's ultimate power?

You cannot do it well enough to exercise your will on God's creation, no matter how tightly you shut your eyes, no matter how your fingers line up, whether you are on your knees or at the dinner table. Just be sure to bow your head in thanksgiving—bow your head in reverence to a power greater than yourself.

Or—open your mouth, not struggling to find the right words, not reaching for the faithful and polished declaration, but trusting that the Spirit intercedes for the saints with sighs too deep for words.

Or—lift up your eyes; lift up your eyes and ask God to open them for once to some hope you've never dared imagine. Reach out your hands and receive a grace that you cannot earn.

"I Wonder Why My Prayers Go Unanswered?"

Charles Reeb • September 18, 2005 • Luke 11:1–13

For many, prayer is understood as an exercise in magic. There are a number of popular religious books out there that seem to support this. People often believe that if they say the right phrases or have the proper technique, they can persuade God to answer their prayers.

But prayer is not rubbing a magic lamp. It is not presenting some Santa Claus in the sky with a list of things we want. Prayer is intimate communication with our Lord. It is as natural as turning around and speaking to a friend. And then, more importantly, it is being quiet and still and listening to God and being transformed by what God is communicating to us. Prayer is vital, for how can we expect to be in relationship with God if we don't communicate with God?

Jesus taught us this lesson. Just read through the Gospel of Luke, and you will find Jesus praying consistently at every turn in his life. He prays as he senses God's call on his life; he prays before choosing his disciples; he prays as he serves and heals other people; he prays as he feels the demands and pressures of his ministry; he prays as he faces the cross; he prays as he finishes his work on the cross. Jesus is continually praying. You could say that prayer for him was as vital as taking his next breath. He knew that in order to live out the life God called him to live, he needed to be continually connected to God in prayer; God was the source of his power.

It was out of his own consistent prayer life that Jesus gives us this teaching in our reading for today. The disciples notice Jesus praying all the time, and they finally get a clue and say, "Teach us to pray." They observe that prayer is a vital practice for Jesus, and they want to learn how to do it. And what follows is a profound lesson from Jesus about prayer. And it is not a lesson in right technique. It is not a lesson in right phrasing. It is not a lesson in how to persuade God. It is a lesson in persistence.

Through the story of the man banging on the door all night, and the repeated words *ask*, *seek*, and *knock*, Jesus is telling us that effective prayer is consistent prayer. Effective prayer is a continual connection to God. And if you look closely at today's scripture you will also notice Jesus telling us that effective prayer is not about what we can *get* from God, but what we *receive* from God. There is a big difference. For oftentimes, what we want from God and what we receive from God are two different things.

We need to keep in mind that what is implied in Jesus's words is that God always answers prayer. Now, God may not give us the answer we want or answer us at the time we want, but God always answers us. And God will always answer us with our best interest at heart. Remember, Jesus said, "If you then, who are evil, know how to give good gifts to your children, how much more will the heavenly Father give the Holy Spirit to those who ask him?" This is a great promise that should encourage us to pray more.

When we ask long enough, seek hard enough, knock loud enough, and pray persistently enough, something happens on the inside of us. The discipline of prayer begins to awaken us to the Holy Spirit inside us, and our motives and desires begin to change. It is as though the persistence of our praying becomes the axe that breaks up the frozen numbness of our souls. Then the power and wisdom of God break in and we begin to be formed by the will of God.

This is what persistent prayer does. It pulls us closer to The Rock, God Almighty. And as we move closer to God in prayer, we find that we do not get what we want from God. We get something better—we get what we need. We get what God wants. We find that as we move closer to our Rock, we begin to desire what God desires, so that what we ask for, knock for, and seek after becomes what God so desperately wants to give us. Then the truth of Jesus's words comes to life so that what we pray for we truly receive. It is a sacred surprise.

"Jesus, Interrupted"

Emily M. Brown • February 12, 2012 • Mark 1:40–45

Too often we get drawn into believing that faithful discipleship means cultivating the correct emotion in our hearts—peaceful contemplation in worship, when truly our minds are roiling with worry; sympathy for a person in need, when truly we are preoccupied with our own concerns; excitement for a mission trip or a life change, when truly we are apprehensive.

When Jesus feels anger and then acts with compassion, he reminds us that discipleship can mean loving God and our neighbor with our actions, *even* when we are angry or anxious or distracted. Discipleship can mean responding faithfully to God's surprises and life's curveballs, even when it is hard. And in that endeavor, friends, we are never alone.

"I wouldn't want to pester God," my Sunday school classmate said years ago. Maybe none of us do. Maybe we all wonder, as the psalmist asked God, "What are human beings that you are mindful of them . . . ?" (Ps. 8:4). What am *I* that you are mindful of *me*? Maybe, like my Sunday school classmate, we fear that we are not important enough to notice, not worthy of God's attention. That might be the reason that so many of us are in such a rush. We are always trying to be more important, to be more productive, to convince ourselves and each other of our own value. We want to be people worthy of attention. But there is nothing we need to do to earn God's attention or God's love.

The promise of this story is that Christ is always ready to turn toward us. On that Galilee road, with so many limits and demands on his time, with so many consequences for stretching out his hand, Jesus chooses to touch and heal because, to Jesus, each one of God's children *matters*. Each one of us is a beloved and beautiful child of God. Each one of us is unique and precious. The good news of this story is that *you matter to God*.

The challenge of this story is to go and do likewise. The challenge is to approach those interruptions and disruptions, those unexpected intrusions and inconvenient crises, those times of uncertainty and change, as moments of opportunity. The challenge is to set aside everything we think we know about God's plan for us, all of our rush and hurry, all of our ideas about who and what is important, and to turn toward our neighbors to bless and heal, to *be* blessed and healed.

Because when we do that, friends, when we take a moment, take a breath, and turn toward each other, we see Jesus with us on the road.

"Do It Yourself"

Beth Birkholz • July 28, 2013 • Luke 11:1–13

When Jesus's disciples came to him and asked him how to pray, he didn't say, "Well, just try it and see how it goes," which is something I've heard myself say sometimes. Jesus didn't give his disciples some long sermon on prayer. What he gave them was very simple and very short.

What a gift the Lord's Prayer is. That's our do-it-yourself manual, right there in the Gospel of Luke. Sometimes I feel like we don't have clear instructions from Jesus on so many things, despite what we hear sometimes in the news. Jesus is, in fact, not clear on many issues of today. But he is clear on what we can say when we talk to God.

It's shorter even than a do-it-yourself video; it's fewer steps than building a patio in your backyard, are the instructions for prayer from Jesus. A little DIY on how to have a relationship with the Creator of the universe, along with some assurance that it is okay to be persistent—and even encouraged—and that God really does *want* to give us good gifts.

So now when people ask how to pray, or say they don't know how to pray or even where to start, I think we can tell them—we can tell ourselves—to start with the very words of Jesus. We have this wonderful, beautiful gift of a do-it-yourself guide on how to pray. It's right there in the Bible and it comes from the one who died and rose again for us, so that we might live as those who have a relationship with God, those who have daily bread, those who have forgiveness, and those who have life.

"In But Not Of the World"

James C. Howell • May 24, 2009 • John 17:6–19

Let's be clear: God doesn't sow cancer cells in people's bodies, God doesn't crash planes into buildings, God doesn't prescribe one child to live under a bridge while my children are in soft beds. God is not in control, or let's say, God does not choose to be in control—because God is love, and love just can't or won't control.

Paul says, "Love does not insist on its own way." God could have made us like marionettes, so God could manipulate us and everything to suit God. But God yearns for our love, and cuts the strings, risking the wounds Jesus was about to incur when he prayed for us.

Understandably, we want everything to go smoothly for us and others, and we associate God with all that is good. But God is the Lord of everything, and in the shadows of that very dark room where Jesus prayed by flickering candlelight for his disciples, we realize he was about to suffer, and the ones he prayed for would suffer too, as all of us face difficulties; some are manageable, some are overwhelming. But Jesus did not promise or even pray for a bubble of safety to envelop us.

In—not of—the world; sanctify them in truth. The truth of the universe is the body, mind, and heart of Jesus. We are not holy, but we can love. And wherever we find ourselves as individuals and as the church, the body, we can say, "In this place, Christ is loved, and you are loved."

We rather feebly reach out to your wounds, and we get it, for we are wounded ourselves, and we touch and we pray, although our prayers may avail little; we know that Jesus prayed so the disciples could see him pray, and he still prays for us now, right now, in heaven. And that is the truth that sanctifies. That is our vocation in the world we are in, and of, but maybe not so much of as we might be.

Questions for Meditation and Discussion

1. When and where do you pray? Do you need silence to pray, or is it possible for you to pray in noisy places? What prevents you from quieting your heart to focus on prayer?

2. What is the relationship between faith and prayer? How can one enhance the other?

3. What are your favorite models of prayer? What draws you to them?

4. Do you ever sing your prayers? Can your favorite hymns or songs be prayers?

5. Who taught you to pray? Who continues to teach you to be a better pray-er?

6. What do you do when you feel as if your prayers are not being answered? How do you know when your prayers have been answered?

7. How important is prayer to your life? During a typical day, how often do you pray? Are there days on which you do not pray? Have you tried praying with a friend or family member? Have you used prayers in the Book of Common Prayer or other resources like it to complement your own prayers? Try it.

8. **GROUP ACTIVITY:** Read aloud together the Lord's Prayer in Luke 11:2–4. Compare the prayer in Luke with the prayer in Matthew 6:9–13. Which one is the more familiar to you? What are the differences and similarities in each prayer? Discuss each verse and its meaning. What is each verse asking? Conclude by praying the Lord's Prayer together.

8 | Peace

Peace. The word itself soothes our weary souls. We breathe it in to fill our hearts, and we exhale all the turmoil and trouble of our life.

But does anything really change? Is peace really possible? And beyond our lives, in a world incessantly torn apart by wars, political conflict, and intractable economic, racial, and social divisions, can we ever live in peace? Can families divided by hurtful words and traumatic actions ever be healed and reunited? What does it take to bring peace to our world? What would a peaceable kingdom really feel like and look like? Do we really want peace, and is peace possible? Does the Bible show us ways to bring peace into our world, and into our lives?

In the Bible, peace in the world is depicted in several ways. Perhaps the best known is in Isaiah 11:6:

> The wolf shall live with the lamb,
> the leopard shall lie down with the kid,
> the calf and the lion and the fatling together,
> and a little child shall lead them.

Isaiah portrays a world in which creatures that are normally enemies will eat and drink together. The larger passage out of which these verses come describes a paradisiacal world filled with the knowledge of the Lord and overflowing with righteousness, love, mercy, and justice. In this passage, at least, peace inverts the order of society so that even the order of the natural world is reversed and returned to its original state of harmony.

Like the writer of the book of Isaiah, Jesus was born into a fragmented world in which political and religious parties struggled to maintain power, often by subjugating some groups of people to other groups of people. Even

Jesus's followers were often divided over their thoughts about his mission in their world. Did he come to bring peace? Did he come to conquer the world with military might? What was their role in his mission?

On one occasion, Jesus and his followers were crossing the sea in a boat when a storm came up, pitching their vessel violently to the point of terrifying the disciples. Of course, Jesus was sound asleep. They woke him, demanding to know if he really cared about them because they were surely perishing. Jesus, perhaps a bit peeved that his friends had woken him for such a pathetic reason, "rebuked the wind, and said to the sea, 'Peace! Be still!'" Like the story in Isaiah, the gospel account imagines a world in which the order of nature is inverted, at least momentarily; such a world is the model of peace.

In that moment, Jesus taught his followers that peace grows out of faithfulness. Having faith that the order of the world can be subverted, having faith that we can help bring about this change through righteous action and deeds, encourages us to move from the stillness of our contemplative prayers to the action of our hands and feet as we move to bring peace to our world.

The *Day1* preachers in this chapter offer some helpful insights and illustrations about what peace in our world today can mean.

"Look to the Child"

John Philip Newell • December 25, 2011 • Luke 2:1–14

The great army of light sings, "Glory to God in the highest, and on earth peace." Do we believe this heavenly pronouncement? Do we really hope for peace on earth, peace in our lives and families, peace among us as religions and nations?

Last year in an interview the Dalai Lama was asked if he had hope for the future. He laughed and said, "Of course I have hope. The future has not yet been decided." Do we believe this? Or do we live as if we believe there is no hope, as if the future has already been determined, as if the fragmentations and divisions of our lives and world are permanent?

At Christmas throughout the world we celebrate the birth of the Child of Peace. Even well beyond the Christian household, men and women with their families and children mark this day with gift-giving and celebration. People and cultures everywhere hear again the song of hope and will look to the Child.

What are the divisions in our lives and communities that we cannot imagine being healed? What is the hatred between religions and nations that we fatalistically assume to be eternal? The future has not yet been decided. Do we believe this? If so, let us turn our creed into deed, our belief into action. Let us reshape the future together.

I invite us today to hear again the song of hope. I call on us as nations to look for the preciousness of the Child in every nation. I call on us as religions to seek the Child's sacredness in every religion. And I call on us as families to be faithful to the healing gifts of the Child in every family. This is the way of love, the way of transformation. Only the power of love will save us, not our love of power. Only love-force will create peace on earth, not brute-force.

The love-force of God is our true soul-force. Shall we open ourselves to what we could never have imagined happening? The Child of Peace can be born again. We carry within us the precious gold of life. We carry within us the sacred fragrance of God. We carry within us the healing salve of love. A new salvation can be born. Do we believe it? If so, let us live it together. "Glory to God in the highest, and on earth peace."

"Our Patience, God's Peace"

Kenneth Carter • December 7, 2008 • Isaiah 40:1–11

Peace. We want peace. But we know so little peace in our world, in our community, in our lives. So, what do we do with this dissonance? How do we resolve it? One response is to say that we are not peaceable people, that we do not really care enough about peace to make it happen. This would be the problem. It's as if we have not figured out a way to construct peace or make it a reality.

But that is not quite right, because peace is not something we can create or invent. We don't always really know what peace is, do we? Some people sentimentalize it. Peace is like a warm blanket or a hot bath or a sedative. Some people compartmentalize peace. I think of the homes in Latin America, in neighborhoods I have walked through, the walls lined with cut glass bottles, the jagged edges exposed to separate those inside from those outside, to keep the peace.

Could we have peace if we just built a gigantic wall? In the land where the Prince of Peace was born, some of his ancestors on both sides have little desire for peace, although the multitudes of Palestinians and Israelis want peace. Could we have peace if we just separated the people we like from the people we don't like? Would that be peace?

It turns out that peace is something different. Here is a definition: peace is a right relationship with God. And a right relationship with God always places us into a right relationship with each other. And here is a further conviction: *We* do not make it a right relationship. *God* has already done that. God has already made peace with the world.

The very absence of peace in our world, the making all things right, has to do with the patience of God, allowing us to use our freedom in God's service, allowing us to use our abundance as the provision of God's blessing, allowing us to use our woundedness as instruments of God's healing.

We are able to wait for peace because we have glimpsed it here and there, now and then; and for the follower of Jesus, the Prince of Peace, something is already growing in us, a hunger and a thirst for a new world. We "wait with a sense of promise."

"Peace amid Bedlam"

Michael Brown • December 13, 2015 • Philippians 4:4–7

Many long years before Jesus was born, in a similar epoch of oppression, a Hebrew prophet had said, "How can we sing peace when there is no peace?" Well, there was no peace in Bethlehem when Jesus was born. But then, isn't that when a Prince of Peace is needed most of all, when there is no peace? That's the kind of world the Prince of Peace was born into then, and the kind of world he is born into even still.

Certainly, the principles of our Christian faith do have the potential, if heard and embraced, to change the world. There is no doubt about that, since those principles replace hatred with grace and violence with the statement, "This is my commandment, that you love one another." But until the world begins to hear and embrace those truths and until it changes—even amid the ongoing bedlam of our Bethlehem existence—there is still another kind of peace available to us, one that passes understanding, one that is more personal than political, and one that gives us the strength to survive whatever the world throws our way.

There are those who say that's too easy, too personal, that it doesn't address the bedlam that is the daily fare of the global masses. But then, as Christians, maybe the path to public peace begins with the individual—with a Prince of Peace who takes our hearts and our hands one at a time and guides us toward our neighbors, in D. T. Niles's words, like "beggars showing other beggars where to find bread." Maybe if I get to know this Messiah amid the bedlam of my own Bethlehem, I will be able to share him with another who will share him with another and another until somehow all their Bethlehems begin to change, too.

That's why we sing, "Let there be peace on earth, and let it begin with me," isn't it? I think Christmas is about that—about Someone who comes in the bedlam of Bethlehem and helps you and me find "a peace that passes understanding," and also helps us pass that peace along, little by little, person by person, encounter by encounter, until at last this old world may well become new.

"Christ the King"

Andrea DeGroot-Nesdahl • November 22, 1998 • 2 Samuel 5:1–5,
Colossians 1:11–20, and John 12:9–19

One lesson from the Christ the King texts is the lesson of peace. Christ's triumph over sin and death gives us peace in all the circumstances we encounter in life. In Colossians, Paul writes about peace coming through the blood of the cross. We understand this to mean that because Christ first suffered and died for us, he gave our suffering, and our dying, new meaning, new value, new perspective. We know because of what he did that we are not alone in our trials. He has gone ahead of us, and yet also remains with us as we walk difficult paths.

That is the miraculous nature of Christ the King. Peace does come through suffering, trauma, or even death to those who follow the King, as we do. God's gift to us in Jesus is the miracle of peace in the face of life's difficulties, large or small peace given even in the face of the final enemy of death.

The triumph of Christ the King is not over governments or rulers, armies or weapons. The triumph of Christ our King is over sin and death. Through the blood of his cross we receive his peace.

"Every Missile Is Aimed at Jesus"

William K. Quick • May 7, 1989 • Luke 2:14,
John 14:27, and Romans 10:15

Jesus promises peace in the gospel. "Peace I leave with you; my peace I give to you." But he goes on to say, "I do not give to you as the world gives" (John 14:27 RSV). I believe Jesus Christ came into the world to show the world the way to peace. I believe God through Christ Jesus ultimately is the One who reigns and who will reign, and that the ways of peace will prevail. However, there is a price for peace. As a people of the Resurrection, we know there is no shortcut to Easter that bypasses Gethsemane and Calvary. Peacemaking is costly.

The tragic fact is that the Christian church has not spoken with a clear witness and convincing voice on the matter of war and peace. Our failure does not acquit us, however, because we are called to be obedient and faithful to the mandate laid upon us as disciples of Christ. We are *to show* the ways of peace, *to proclaim* the ways of peace, *to be peacemakers* not just peace talkers. This call is true for the Christian in all areas of life—not just war and peace. All relationships within life are covered by this summons.

We need to take steps that lead to peace. Pastors and laity are not tactical experts, but when initiatives for peace are taken, we should show our willingness to risk in order to build a basis of trust.

It is never enough to proclaim the good news. Christians must be risktakers. It is never enough to pray for peace if we are unwilling to take the initiative, to show our willingness to take first steps, to lose ourselves for the sake of the gospel in order to bring about the unity and reconciliation between peoples and nations.

America needs to export wonder-working values instead of wonder-working weapons. We are all things to all people because we like it that way. Have we been seduced more by a love of power than by the power of love? Have we, as Christians, become more concerned about *projecting an image* than we are in *reflecting an Image*?

Christians are an alternative community to a society based on power. All around the world America is seen as being on the defensive. We need to take the offensive, seize the initiative, show our willingness to take those first steps. Christians are called to be the Lord's vanguard. If we don't take the initiative, who will? If Christians cannot model the ways of Jesus for the world, the way to reconciliation that bridges communities and brings meaning to people's lives, who will? Let the grassroots effort at peacemaking begin with us.

Let us dare to believe and pray, work and risk, to convince the church and the world, "The God of life calls us all; turn away from the path of death and choose life."

"Peacemaking in a Nuclear Age"

Thomas L. Jones • September 21, 1986 • Isaiah 2:1–5
and Romans 12:1, 9, 14–21

Everybody is for "peace." But what does that mean? Recently, I have really been struggling with that. And it is not an easy struggle. Today, my hope is to begin a continuing struggle for you and those who talk to you to know what you believe, why you believe it, and help each other to the courage to do a "here I stand" on the basis of thought-out and prayed-out conviction. We need to spur each other on in the pilgrimage to know about peacemaking and to become better peacemakers.

My present pilgrimage in the faith has now convicted me:

1. Non-violence is the way and will of God. One cannot take the Sermon on the Mount, nor the rest of the New Testament, seriously and be violent. Jesus rejected violence for any reason. The Christian doctrine of love, operating through the method of non-violence, is the most potent weapon available in the struggle to overcome oppression. Such a stand is not to acquiesce, but to proclaim in positive ways that the love of God let loose in the world is the most powerful force the world can ever know. I believe we have reached a point unlike any in history where we must choose

faith in God and the moral power of God controlling God's universe, or else. As Jim Wallis writes, "The church is having its vocation radicalized."

2. I am convinced that non-violence is practical. It does work. It will not accomplish miracles overnight. Immediately it does give self-respect to those committed to it. Non-violence does stir the conscience of opponents that reconciliation is possible. Love is the only force capable of transforming an enemy into a friend. Jesus was non-violent and ended up on a cross, but to judge that as a failure is to deny the victorious power of the Resurrection. Because we are bound to Christ, we can overcome our wish to be secure, and we can leave behind, as superfluous, our requirement for violence. Then we are free to love one another.

3. I am convinced that in this struggle we must realize fully that means are not to be distinguished from ends. If violent means are used, there will be bad results. Evil means, even for a good end, produce evil results. A world motivated by using the majority of the world's resources to provide violent deterrents may not be worth saving anyway.

4. I believe that, in a dark, confused world, the Kingdom of God may yet reign in the hearts of humanity. We are being forced to consider a deeper faith than ever before. In that faith is opportunity to experience in deeper ways than ever that the universe is under the control of a loving purpose: God is real; God is a living God; God promises "I will be with you"; God does not break promises. The issue is one of faith—whether we place our national security in weaponry or in God. We will not have a peace movement if it does not come out of a deep Christian faith.

5. I am convinced that any commitment to non-violence must begin with the way I live my own life. I will not protect myself with violent means. I have never had a gun so that is not where I need to start. However, Christian commitment

does demand a stance about that. But there are other subtle and devious ways violence tempts and controls me. I need the help of those around me to work to overcome any violent ways by which I treat other persons by reacting in defensive, manipulative, tyrannical, or other dominating self-serving ways, instead of acting in Christian love and grace.

We need to commit that, in the pilgrimage we begin today toward helping each other understand and be Christian peacemakers in a nuclear age, we not do violence to each other by trying to force positions on each other—but rather, in love, struggle toward deeper commitments out of faith in God revealed in Christ.

"Peace—I Got This"

Kate Moorehead • April 8, 2018 • John 20:19–31

Jesus said something really important when he appeared in the Gospel of John. In fact, he repeats the same phrase three times. And if Jesus repeats something three times, you know it must be important because he didn't repeat himself much at all. Most of the time, he says things only once and you have to hang onto his every word. But this time, Jesus says that same greeting three times—twice in this one appearance and again when he appears to the group with Thomas present. He says, "Peace be with you."

Jews did use the phrase *shalom aleichem* to greet one another. But for Jesus to say this three times, I believe that he was trying to tell us something. And Christians all over the world believe this too, for we all say, "The Peace of the Lord be with you," as our final words before we receive communion. We don't think much about it; we call it "The Peace." But we do say these words to one another because, when Jesus appeared in resurrected form, this is what he said.

But what does it really mean: *Peace be with you*? I think that in order to understand what Jesus meant, we have to look deep inside ourselves, deep in that place where fear resides. If you found yourself all alone on a huge mountain, no idea where you were, one of the first feelings we would have would be very reasonable because, as human beings, we are geared for survival. So, our first and most primal emotion would be fear. We are afraid of being lost, of dying, of pain, of suffering, of change. Heck, when it comes down to it, we are afraid most of the time. We just have other words for it now so it doesn't make us feel so bad. We use these words for different kinds of fear—stress, anxiety, worry. Even anger or depression are related to fear. They are cousins.

Peace, for the believer in Christ, has nothing to do with what is going on around you. Peace is a state of awareness. It is not a feeling and it is not dependent on the circumstances of your life. Peace is a mystical awareness that transcends time and space. No matter what is going on in your life, you can access this peace that Jesus gave us when he came to us after the resurrection. It is his gift to you.

Peace is the pure awareness that Jesus is your Savior. That you have been saved and that Jesus is saving you even now.

Peace is the awareness that *Jesus has got this.* He has done it. It is done for you. Nothing can take away God's love for you. Nothing. It is done. You are loved. You are alive. You are held. You are not alone.

Questions for Meditation and Discussion

1. How do you define peace? Is peace simply the absence of conflict? Is it possible to define peace without thinking about conflict?

2. Where do you find peace in your life? What spiritual disciplines help you to achieve peace?

3. How does following Jesus provide peace for us?

4. Numerous biblical passages depict peace and ways to achieve it, and many of those passages are discussed in the sermons in this chapter. As you think about having peace in your life or peace in the world, which scriptures speak most profoundly to you, and why?

5. Did Jesus come to bring about a kingdom of peace? What did peace mean for Jesus?

6. A famous painting by American painter Edward Hicks is titled *The Peaceable Kingdom*; its images are drawn from Isaiah 11:1–9. Find an image of the painting and look at its details. How well does it evoke and portray the details of the Isaiah passage? How is such a kingdom possible?

7. Several gospel songs and hymns focus on peace: "Peace Like a River," "I've Got Peace in My Heart," "It Is Well with My Soul." Select one or two of your favorite hymns about peace and listen to several versions of them. Use these during your meditation time as you reflect on the meaning of peace in your own life. Focus on the images of peace in the songs. How do the songs describe peace?

8. **GROUP ACTIVITY:** Should Christians be pacifists? Do the gospels present Jesus as a peacemaker? Divide into small groups to discuss ways that Christians have responded to wars throughout history, but especially in recent history. Should Christians avoid all conflicts with the state? Many politicians say that peace can only be achieved through war and speak of a "Just War." Is it ever possible to achieve peace through war? Share your conclusions together, and close with the prayer attributed to St. Frances, "Lord, make me an instrument of your peace."

9 | Justice

"And justice for all." These days we so glibly toss about that phrase that we are no longer sure what we mean by the word justice. Do we mean that justice and equality are synonymous? That is, are people with few resources treated the same way as people who have more resources so that all people are treated equally? What about racial injustice and systemic racism? Does justice refer simply to legal justice, or does it also refer to economic justice and social justice? And are we referring to retributive justice or to distributive justice? What is the relationship between justice and love? Does loving our enemies and praying for them require treating them justly? Can we practice "just mercy"?

The Bible offers many examples of people struggling with questions about justice. In the Gospel of Luke, Jesus sits down to speak with a group of Jewish leaders who question him about keeping various purity laws. Following a few rounds of questions, Jesus responds, "You . . . neglect justice and the love of God" (Luke 11:42). In his teachings and his deeds, Jesus demonstrates that justice requires more than simply a blind and unwavering acceptance of the letter of every law. When we are consumed with following every little detail of the laws, we neglect those around us whom God loves and who need our attention.

Loving others may sometimes require forgoing strict adherence to the laws so that we may act with love and mercy toward others, and thus truly practice justice. Jesus provides the greatest example of one who acts with just mercy toward those who have been neglected by the social and religious systems of his day.

Plenty of biblical stories depict the struggle to define justice. In the book of Job, a "blameless and upright man" experiences horrific and inexplicable suffering: he loses all his wealth when all his livestock die; he is devastated by illness; his children all die. His distraught wife encourages him to curse God and die, but Job—at least in the early chapters of the book—responds that God is just, for both good and evil come from the hands of God.

As the story progresses, a very different set of possible answers to the question of justice develops. His friends tell Job that he must indeed have broken some threads in the social and religious fabric around him. Maybe he didn't sacrifice correctly when his children did something wrong; maybe he committed a crime; maybe his parents did something he's now suffering for. Job refuses to accept any of these explanations and asks to speak directly to God. When Job gets that opportunity, he asks God why he is suffering so unjustly. God never answers Job's questions directly, but instead points to the created order. In the end, Job recognizes God's greatness as Creator, and his health, wealth, and family are restored. Yet, does Job receive justice? Where does he find justice?

Perhaps the most familiar biblical passage about justice comes from Micah 6:8:

> *What does the Lord require of you but to do justice, and to love kindness, and to walk humbly with your God?*

The prophet Micah utters these words after a series of questions about the ways that individuals should be righteous before God. Do righteousness and correct worship of God require external shows of holiness such as public prayer, the public giving of tithes, or public attendance at temple? No, declares the prophet, who is the mouthpiece for God; righteousness requires walking humbly with God and acting with justice, mercy, and loving-kindness with others. For Micah, the requirements of being righteous are simple, even though they are not easy to practice daily.

The *Day1* preachers in this chapter offer helpful insights into the questions of justice, and remind us how important the practice of justice is in developing communities of faith.

"A Rediscovery of Biblical Religion"

Daniel Vestal • December 28, 2003 • Micah 6:8

Biblical religion is justice, mercy, and walking humbly with God. It is the essence of biblical faith and the great need in the church of Jesus Christ. But how do we do it? How does all of this become more than rhetoric or sentiment or wishful thinking? How do justice, love, and walking with God become a way of life?

Well, let me suggest that biblical religion becomes a way of life only after profound and continuous conversion—conversion made possible by the grace of our Lord Jesus Christ, the love of God, and the fellowship of the Holy Spirit.

God did not wait until the coming of Christ to send the message of equality and justice to the people. God sent it at the creation. Humanity as created by God is already capable of understanding that one must not live on the blood of the poor and that white skin is not more precious than black.

But not only must our hearts be changed if justice and mercy are to become a way of life; our minds must also be changed. For most of us, our thinking is shaped more by popular culture, family, and friends than it is by Christ. We think with the prevailing prejudices that surround us. We harbor the same stereotypes and have the same blind spots as everyone else, and so our way of thinking needs conversion.

So, if justice and mercy and walking humbly with God are to become a way of life, our hearts must change. Our minds must change. Our behavior must change. In biblical religion, belief and practice come together. Heart and mind and behavior are in concert with one another. Justice, mercy, and walking with God are intensely personal before they are social, and they are the result of spiritual transformation.

God's desire for the church is for us to be so changed that we become a burning bush that is aflame with the glory of God. God's desire for each one of us is to be so changed that we become a river of living water out of which life and joy floods to others. God's desire for the church and for us individually is to be so changed that we become a people who are passionate about justice and mercy and who discover how to walk humbly with God.

"The Power of Today"

Diana Butler Bass • January 24, 2016 • Luke 4:14–21

Jesus essentially told his friends, "Look around. See the Spirit of God at work, right here. Right now. God is *with us.* Just as I AM promised our father Moses at the burning bush, 'I will be with you.' This is the sign of God's covenant. The ever-active, ever-loving, ever-liberating, always present God is here with us. Now."

In effect, Jesus is asking his friends to open their eyes, to see the burning bush, to become more attentive to God's promise to abide with Israel in the land, and that God is keeping God's promise no matter how awful the outward circumstances. This is not a call toward quiescence—meditate and everything else will go away. Instead, it is a call to see more deeply, past the immediate sin, injustice, trials, and evils of human life to the profound reality of love and compassion upon which everything else truly rests: the love of God and neighbor.

If we can *see, experience, and grasp* that the active force of love is at work in the world now, our fear recedes, our hatreds melt, our willingness to murder and kill and seek revenge flows away with the tide, and we can recognize that in the midst of all things—even in the worst oppression—God is with us. Through our delusions of domination, the clarity of grace, mercy, and justice make themselves known to us. And that transforms fear into compassion, giving us the power to walk in the way of love God intended.

In a very real way, the Spirit was upon Jesus. But it was also upon his friends and neighbors, too. For Jesus was one of them. And by emphasizing the word *today*, Jesus transformed Isaiah's words, Isaiah's prophecy, into a powerful invitation for the whole community to act on behalf of God's justice. The text might have read:

> The Spirit of the Lord is upon me (and therefore also with you), because he has anointed us to bring good news to the poor. He has sent us to proclaim release to the captives and recovery of sight to the blind, to let the oppressed go free, to proclaim the year of the Lord's favor.

Living in God's promise is not about yesterday. Nor is it about awaiting some distant Messiah and eternal life in the Kingdom of God. It is about *now*. This is a hard truth to hear and receive. Jesus's friends refused. They would rather stay mired in nostalgia and complain about the future. How great the prophets were! If only a savior would appear and get us out of this mess!

But Jesus's sermon remains as clear and poignant and important and urgent as ever: *Today* this promise has been fulfilled in your hearing—what we need is here. Today.

"A New World Birthed"

Walter Brueggemann • December 19, 2004 • Matthew 1:18–25

The Bible is largely a reflection on how God's Spirit makes things new.

It is God's Spirit in Genesis 1 that creates a new world, a new heaven, and a new earth. It is God's Spirit, God's wind, that blows the waters back in Egypt and lets our ancestors depart from slavery. It is God's Spirit that calls prophets and apostles and martyrs to do dangerous acts of obedience. It is God's Spirit that came upon the disciples in the Book of Acts and created a community of obedience and mission. And now, it is God's Spirit that begins something new when the world is exhausted, when our imagination fails, and when our lives are shut down in despair.

That is what Matthew is telling us, that God's Spirit has stirred and caused something utterly new in the world. God has caused this new baby who will change everything among us.

Notice that the angel gives Joseph two names for the baby. Names are very important in that ancient world. First, the angel says, "You shall call his name *Jesus*, for he will save his people." The Hebrew name *Jesus* is the verb *save*. Imagine on Christmas that we have a baby named *Save*. Many babies in the Old Testament are named *Save*. It is the word for Joshua, for Isaiah, and for Hosea. Each of them saved Israel, and now Jesus will save.

Jesus will save from sin and guilt. Jesus will save from death and destruction. Jesus will save from despair and hopelessness. Jesus will save from poverty and sickness and hunger, and in all of the stories of Jesus that the church remembers, it is Jesus who saves.

The second name that the angel gives for the baby is *Emmanuel*, God is with us. It is the faith of the church that in Jesus, God was decisively present in the world that made everything new. And in the New Testament we have all of that evidence that wherever Jesus came, he showed up where people were in need and he saved them—lepers, the deaf, the blind, the lame, the hungry, the unclean, even the dead. His very presence makes new life possible, and the church consists in all the people who have been dazzled by the reality of God who has come to be with us in this season of need and of joy, all through this miraculous baby.

So Matthew gives us an angel's message in a dream that is beyond our control or expectation. He tells us that it is God's Spirit who makes all things new through this baby, and he names the baby twice. The baby is named *Save*, and Jesus saves from all that kills and is flat and sad. He names the baby *God is with us*, and we are not alone.

Notice that this story does not ask us to do anything. But I believe it invites us to be dazzled. It invites us to ponder that, while our world feels unsavable, here is the baby named *Save*. Our world and our lives often feel abandoned, and here is the baby named *God is with us*. So we are to be ready to have our lives and our world contradicted by this gift from God. We may rest our lives upon the new promise from the angel, and we may be safe and we may be whole and made generous, because Christmas is coming soon.

"The Mind of Christ"

Leontine Kelly • April 5, 1998 • Luke 22:14–23, 56

When marking Palm Sunday, as we wave the branch of palms or wear the neatly cut crosses made from the palm, we are called to remember not only the drama of the day, but also the purpose of the day—so that we, with renewed minds and hearts, can by the depth of God's love for us transform the world.

A procession this past summer brought *Alleluia!* and *Praise God!* to my lips. Hundreds of children, parents, and adult escorts marched thirty miles on a Children's Crusade to Death Row from the Bruderhof Community of Farmington, Pennsylvania, to the State Correctional institution in Waynesburg. There they demonstrated—with prayer, songs, and speeches—against the use of capital punishment in the United States.

The record of this event is included in an editorial of *Christian Social Action* under the heading "End Capital Punishment, Celebrate Life Instead," in commemorating the life, death, and resurrection of Jesus, who came to give life—abundant life to all. The words of Jonathan Kozol to the Bruderhof children call renewal in the mind of Christ:

> In this benighted nation that denies food to the poor while it finds money it needs to build new prisons, it is fitting that children lead us in that search for our salvation. The death chamber is our national sacrilege and shame. It celebrates murder by the state, betrays the gospel, and tramples on the scriptures. The children's crusade celebrates life.

May we have the mind of Jesus Christ.

"The Church: The Glorious Liberty of the Children of God"

Patricia McClurg • June 25, 1978 • Matthew 12:46–50

God liberates us from sin—that state of being out of harmony with God and out of harmony with us. And God liberates us from the consequences of sin—the oppressing, the grinding down, the limiting, the stunting of the growth of anyone who is human. God calls us into a new family, where there is abundant life, where there are whole, healthy people, women and men, living up to their full potential.

The early church grew even among, and especially among, those of the lower class of society—those who were called *slave* and those who were called *women*. And the reverberations of that revolution, that planting of the Lord, go on yet today. Something happens in that new family life in Christ that abolishes differences that divide us and thwart our development as human beings. Something happens in that new family "in the Lord" that makes us all mutually interdependent with one another and with him. To be a part of this family called the people of God is to be a part of beating down, overcoming, the limitations that sin and culture have placed upon us.

Liberty—not to be confined or oppressed, good tidings, Good News of what God has done, is doing, and will surely accomplish. We await and press on toward the grand finale in confident hope. The new family. The new age working itself out in these states of ours and around the planet Earth.

That day long ago in Nazareth, Jesus brought encouragement, a view of the future that has given centuries of people the endurance and the hardheaded hope that will see us through to the fulfillment of Isaiah's dream of the day when the lion and the lamb will lie down together, when the sinful inclination of the strong to devour the weak will be no more.

This is no free-falling, no free-floating liberation—there is nothing libertine about it. It is a binding liberation, issuing in a new family which requires mutual commitment, the recognition of mutual dependence, of a shared suffering and of the power of love to knit together all parts of the body. A community intimately bound together in which there is neither Jew nor Gentile, slave nor master, male nor female. A community of righteousness which reaches out to help and incorporate those who have had their rights taken away from them. Freedom from fear, freedom from that which deforms human life, from that which inhibits. And freedom for that which binds us together as sisters and brothers.

"Justice Denied— Except from the God of Love"

David Gushee • April 29, 2018 • Psalm 22:25–31; 1 John 4:7–21; John 15:1–8

On a daily basis, human life is about power—who has it and who doesn't, who can humiliate others and who faces humiliation, who sets the terms of welcome and who faces the back of the hand and the close of the door. It appears to be one of sinful humanity's greatest pleasures, this exercise of power to the exclusion of others.

But the psalmist knows that human powers only think they are in charge. Dominion truly belongs to the Lord; God rules over the nations. There is a fundamental human equality in this—God rules all, and all who live, and all who die, shall answer to God. All who sleep in the earth—the Hebrew here suggests especially all who sleep well, in their comfort and power—these shall bow down, down, down before the God who is ruler of all, equally of all, the God who shatters all human pretensions to power and majesty.

Our text from 1 John speaks not of justice but of love. But here justice and love are not in contradiction. It is precisely because the God we have met in Jesus Christ is so clearly a God of love that claims about God's coming justice make so much sense.

God is love, says John. Love is God's defining characteristic. This divine love was decisively revealed in God's decision to send Jesus into the world to be the atoning sacrifice for human sins—and to give us a new kind of life, now and eternally, in and through Jesus.

If we abide in Christ, we too can over time learn to love in the same way—freely and unconditionally. So often it is fear that causes our impulse to gain, hold, and abuse power over others, to draw lines as to who is in and who is out, even to crush those whom we find most strange, most threatening, most *other*—that pattern that Psalm 22 suggests leads straight to the judgment of God.

These John texts show a better way: abide in Jesus, the Son of God, who takes away the sins of the world, and who incarnates the love of God as no one before or since. Abide in him. Drink deeply of his love. In that tender love is no fear. Born of that tender love is a fierce desire to create a world in which no more people have their faces crushed into the dust by the boot of oppression.

Questions for Meditation and Discussion

1. How do you define justice? Do you find the word justice to be used in different ways, for different purposes, in our society? Why do you think that is?

2. How does Jesus practice justice? Can you describe some of the stories that depict Jesus embodying justice?

3. What is the last act of justice you witnessed? What impact did it have on you?

4. Does the church engage in justice today? In what ways does it practice justice? Are there ways in which it does not practice justice?

5. Is God a just God? Can you describe what this question means to you? How do you define the justice of God? Can you think of examples from the Bible that depict God as a just God?

6. What exactly is "just mercy"? What is the relationship between love, mercy, and justice? How might that relationship play out in our own daily lives?

7. How do you "do justice, love kindness, and walk humbly with your God" together as a church? What are some ideas you might have to practice that as a congregation in your community?

8. **GROUP ACTIVITY:** Discuss the various types of justice practiced in our society. How does society's justice reflect biblical justice? How may it be different? How can we work together to bring biblical justice into our world?

10 | Church

When Jesus said to his disciple Peter, "You are Peter, and on this rock I will build my church, and the gates of Hades will not prevail against it" (Matthew 16:18), could he have imagined the challenges the church would face through history?

The New Testament and other early church documents depict an ideal church whose head is Christ and whose members assent to creedal statements that provide the contours of a community of faith, as well as to establish the orthodoxy—right belief—of these communities. However, as with any other group in human society, the church has always faced challenges from within and without. As with any other organization composed of individuals with different desires, dreams, hopes, and wishes, conflict can erupt in the church as some seek to promote their wishes over others'.

As a result, when people look at the church from the outside they often see in-fighting and indecision and an inability of some to get along with others. And when people inside the church look at themselves, they often see the same kinds of divisiveness, though they ask themselves continually about their mission in the world: Shouldn't we be able to love one another as Jesus loved us so that we can show the world outside the church the love of Jesus? Whatever happened to "They'll Know We Are Christians by Our Love"?

Even in the earliest churches, members struggled to define themselves as well as to identify themselves over other religious movements of the time. Many struggled with their purpose, and with questions of membership— who should we let into our community? In the twenty-first century, many Christians look back on the early church with fondness and point to it as a unified community whose message was pure and its unity pristine. Despite such an idyllic portrait, the earliest Christian communities were often as rife with disagreement as contemporary Christian communities—just read Paul's epistles. In addition, there was not a single "early church," but a diversity of Christian communities, each of which held their versions of creedal statements that addressed their own cultural contexts.

In contemporary culture, the church continues to ponder its role in society, perhaps more so now than ever. In years past, churches spoke with distinctive voices in dialogue with political organizations and social movements. In the mid-twentieth century, churches witnessed growth in membership and subsequent organizational growth—and *The Protestant Hour* radio program was proof of that. In the early years of the twenty-first century, in contrast, church membership has continued to decline; leaders and members ponder ways to restore interest in church, as well as to demonstrate the value of church for a generation of people whose families may not have been a part of a faith community before.

The *Day1* preachers in this chapter address the role of the church in contemporary society and provide sustenance regarding the relationships between Jesus and the church, and between church and culture.

"How Big Is the Church?"

Dock Hollingsworth • May 7, 2017 • Acts 2:42–47

One day, Peter got up to preach and there were people there from every region—Parthians, Medes, Elamites, and residents of Mesopotamia. Peter preached the Resurrection story and three thousand people were added to the rolls of the church. In one day, the church went from the size of a Sunday school class to a three-thousand-member mega-church.

It was a risky design for a church start. Jesus left the faithful without a building, without a constitution and bylaws, without committees or even a pastor. Jesus left them no staff or structure, no budget or mission project. Tough start—but Jesus did leave them with each other. To start with, they had the presence of the Holy Spirit and each other, and that's it.

Acts tells the story of how they structured themselves and formed the soul of the early church: "They devoted themselves to the apostles' teaching and fellowship, to the breaking of bread and to the prayers." And they began a tradition of sharing their possessions with those who were less fortunate.

Their core activities were teaching, fellowship, breaking of bread, prayers, and giving. Does this seem a little internally focused? There is no mention of mission—no mention of a ministry to a hurting world. They were giving, sharing their possessions, but it was all distributed within the community. The church's mission forms later, but first they gathered themselves into Christian community. Until they learned to care for each other, they were not going to be much help to the larger world.

Teaching, fellowship, breaking of bread, prayers, and giving. This early church covenant sounds so simplistic, yet every church around the globe that is getting it right has rooted itself back into these simple disciplines.

I have come to learn that there are congregations all over the planet that have taken a sprig from this early Palestinian church and used it to replant—and the same thing grew again. All over there are faith communities that tie their history back to this same beginning, rooted in this same story, and they gather every week and do the same things and it makes them—as we say here in the South—our kinfolk; they are our brothers and sisters and first cousins because we share a family tree.

When I was growing up in my little home church, I did not understand that I had these relatives who were tied to the same story and beginnings and commission. I have come to learn how big the church is—and now if I enter a church in Boston or Bursa or Bucksnort, I am greeted with the same hugs that we share at the Hollingsworth family reunion. The older I get, the more impressed I become with the size of this common church.

Since the day of Peter's sermon, the church has grown to the Parthians, Medes, Elamites, and dwellers of Mesopotamia—which means we have kinfolk everywhere. Listening to *Day1* is a reminder of that larger family. I hear preachers from Chicago and St. Paul, and they preach about fellowship and communion and prayer and giving, and I know we share the same great-grandparents.

There is a chance that you listen to *Day1* but are not part of a local congregation. You might think the next one could never be as good as the last one. Or, you might have been hurt by a church that got off mission. Try again. All across the globe there are families of faith that are getting it right. But I will warn you, if they are getting it right, they will ask you to give away your money and eat together and share the Lord's Table together and study and pray together. And thanks be to God. Thanks be to God for the churches that are getting it right.

"A Great Time to Be the Church"

Patrick Keen • June 15, 2008 • Matthew 9:35–10:1

There have been many times in the history of the church for the church to manifest itself as the body of Christ. There have been times when the church has stood up to the challenge, and times when the church has utterly failed.

As we re-remember the pictures of the people of God in post-Katrina New Orleans wading in the flood waters, as we listened to the stories of them skirmishing for food and fresh water, as we remember visuals of the elderly and young babies in the ninety-degree heat of the August sun waiting for help to come, there was no help. We saw people standing on the roofs of their houses waiting to be rescued, many dying from heat exhaustion and dehydration. Many more died than will ever be reported. It was an embarrassment to us as a nation. The world watched as our federal government failed to respond. They watched as our state government failed to act. They watched as our city government was crippled and unable to do anything but cry out for help.

Well, the church responded to that cry for help. The church saw and responded like never before, sending help in the form of gift cards, in the form of money donated to every entity that claimed to be raising money on behalf of those who were victimized by this horrific disaster that has been categorized as the worst natural disaster to ever hit this nation.

The ecumenical church, the church universal, came forth as the body of Christ to minister to the needs of this devastated people as they were moved to every state in the country. The church opened its arms and doors to welcome them into their communities and helped to provide new starts for those who had become displaced.

The church ecumenical has done so much to help so many over the past years. But if you were to visit, you would find that there is still so much more to be done. There are opportunities for the church to be that visible witness of the kingdom of God in ways that our best preachers could never put in the most eloquent of words.

This is a call to discipleship. This is an opportunity for you to be that disciple to whom Christ has given authority to bring help, health, hope, and wholeness to those who are marginalized in this region of our nation and indeed around the world. You have been commissioned. Will you go?

This is a great time to be the church.

"Come and See What Found Me!"

Kevin Strickland • January 19, 2020 • John 1:29–42

We are called to invite others to "come and see." To come and see God in Christ made manifest in bread and wine, water and word, forgiven sinners and welcomed strangers.

What might our churches look like—and our own faith lives—if we lived fully knowing that we have been found by a God who loves us completely and calls us to ventures at times where we can't even see the ending, but knowing God's hand is guiding us?

What might our churches look like—and our own faith lives— if we believed that inviting someone to "come and see" how God's grace is for everyone and how it will completely change one's life, if you let it?

We often make inviting others into the faith far more complicated than it needs to be, and even our own living into that invitation, far more complicated. God's story shifts our focus away from our own efforts to get others to see Jesus and reminds us that we are able to see only because God has first revealed Godself to us. We see because we have been seen and love because we have first been loved. In Jesus, we can trust that God sees us, and in the redemptive line of God's sight we have new life.

Those of us who are followers of Jesus in a highly skeptical if not downright hostile environment can learn from Andrew the disciple, who reminds us that our calling is to bear witness with grace and obedience to the light that shines on our lives through the Son of God. The ability of others to see that light does not rest solely on our powers of theological persuasion, our skills of fancy biblical language or technology, our ability to communicate in culturally relevant ways, or even our sheer persistence. Rather, the ability to see Jesus comes as a gift from God through the graceful and mysterious movements of the Holy Spirit.

We can take others by the hand, share our excitement with them, and invite them by the faithful living of our lives to come and get a glimpse of what we've seen—but we cannot make them see. We make sure that our lives are pointed toward the light, and then live in the daring trust that the light shines and the darkness will not overcome it.

"The Woman Who Just Said No"

Anna Carter Florence • November 11, 2007 • Esther 1:1–2:4

I would be willing to bet good money that in your family there are plenty of stories, some of which have been classified as dangerous—which means that certain relatives would rather not think about them, let alone pass down to the children. Sometimes there are good reasons for keeping things quiet. Maybe it's better the kids don't know how Aunt Tess kept her family together or how Great Grandpa made his money or how Uncle John survived the war. Maybe so. But, sometimes, dangerous memories stop being dangerous when we get them out in the open and learn from them. Sometimes, they can make a family stronger.

The church is a family just like any other. It has stories, sacred stories, many of them collected in our Bible. And just like any other family, sometimes the church considers its sacred stories to be dangerous memories, and it takes them out of circulation, so to speak. That's why you haven't heard much about Vashti. The church has traditionally seen her story as a dangerous memory, so she isn't in the lectionary of assigned readings.

Now for someone like me, that's just an invitation to turn on the searchlights. What's so dangerous about Queen Vashti? After all, the writer of the book of Esther thought she was important enough to remember; she is in the Bible. So why haven't we heard more about her?

On another level, however, the story of Vashti cannot be erased. There are echoes of her great *no* reverberating all through the Bible. Vashti may be nothing but a prologue to the book of Esther in the church's eyes for all that we hear about her, but in the Bible she lives on in the minds of her people, the king, and most importantly, Queen Esther herself.

Maybe the church has thought that Vashti challenges the order of the day in a dangerous way. She does, after all, say *no* to the king. What if everyone said *no* to the king? What if every woman said *no* to a man? Maybe the church has not wanted us to consider a world in which subjects just say *no* to their leaders and women just say *no* to men.

And maybe the church has missed the point. After all, the king in this story hardly asks his wife to fetch his slippers; he demands that she do something unthinkable and humiliating, something which totally violates the marriage contract. Are we supposed to obey things that compromise our integrity? Is this what we teach our daughters and our sons?

I think the church has traditionally been so upset by the male-female dynamics in this story that it has forgotten to look further than the royal feud between king and queen. This story is about more than that. It is not merely a feminist message. It is not a story for women looking for a reason to rebel. This is a story for every person who has ever felt their integrity called into question, who has ever had to weigh the risks between their job and their self-respect, who has ever had to stand up in the face of an unjust situation and say, "*No*, I cannot go along with this."

I wonder what would happen if we put the story of Vashti back into circulation. Would our children have a role model for just saying *no* to adults who try to molest or harm them? Would our daughters muster a little more courage for just saying *no* to a boyfriend who keeps pressuring them to have sex when they don't want to? Would it give you and me a place to begin talking about the hundreds of awkward, troubling moments in our lives when we feel like we are being asked to do something that puts our integrity at risk? The boss tells us to hide money in a fake expense account, or a friend at a party offers us drugs that we don't want, or a family member assumes that we'll keep ignoring the addiction that's ruining his life and ours.

Things can and do happen every day that challenge our integrity. What do we do? Do we just say *no*? It isn't easy.

"The Body of Christ Takes Up Space on Earth"

Barbara K. Lundblad • May 12, 1996 • John 14:1–14

In the Upper Room, Jesus promised to be present with the disciples in a different way. "I will ask my Father, and he will give you another Advocate, to be with you forever." But forever was not postponed to a time after death; forever included life on this earth. The Spirit of truth, the Advocate, will come here. Jesus's presence will be deeper than memory and closer than heaven. That is, Jesus will forever be messed up with this body life, this earthiness which some tell us to discount, even disdain.

Though Jesus's promise is surely personal, it is primarily communal. These words are Jesus's last words to the community he has gathered, the community of disciples that would become the church. Now, I realize that you are not listening to this in church—you're in an apartment or a house or in your car. You may have no intention of being part of any church (because church is too boring or too destructive or too full of hypocrites or too whatever). Maybe if the church were pure spirit, it would be more satisfying.

Dietrich Bonhoeffer was a Lutheran pastor who was hanged for his part in a plot to kill Hitler. In his book *Costly Discipleship*, he wrote about Christ's body, the church. "The body of Christ takes up space on the earth," he said—as buildings take up space, also cars, dirt, flowers, rocks, skateboards, and people. Then Bonhoeffer goes on, "A truth, a doctrine, or a religion needs no space for themselves. They are disembodied entities . . . that is all. But the incarnate Christ needs not only ears or hearts but living people who will follow him." The body of Christ takes up space on the earth. This is more than a spiritual metaphor; it is bodily reality.

Which is why we are often so dissatisfied with the church: if the church didn't take up space, it (or we) could be more faithful. If it were spiritual instead of earthy, we could do those things Jesus promised the disciples long ago. Still Jesus calls us to claim space on the earth, to remain here, to do the kingdom's work begun in Galilee.

Those of us who are part of the church know we are not what Jesus called us to be. We spend too much and share too little; we judge too many and love too few; we wait too long and act too late. Perhaps you are saying, "Show me a church where ministers aren't self-serving, where hypocrisy has been purged away, where love is genuine, and I'll become a member." You'll wait a long time, my friend, for such a church takes up no space on this earth. It has floated up, up, up and disappeared beyond Oz. Or perhaps, such a church lives as a memory—a time when disciples believed, when faith could move mountains, and motives were pure.

Who shall ascend into the hill of the Lord? Or who shall stand in God's holy space? There is no one but us. There is no one to send, nor a clean hand, nor a pure heart on the face of the earth, but only us, a generation comforting ourselves with the notion that we have come at an awkward time, that our innocent ancestors are all dead and our children are busy and troubled, and we ourselves unfit, not yet ready, having each of us chosen wrongly, made a false start, failed, yielded to pressure, and grown exhausted. But there is no one but us. There never has been. There have been generations that remembered, and generations that forgot; there has never been a generation of whole men and women who lived well for even one day.

There is no one but us, not in this time and space. The twelve disciples are gone and heaven is not yet here. I trust Jesus's promise about the dwelling places in God's house, about a future with Jesus that I cannot see. But do I, do you, also trust the promise that the Spirit has come now to this earth? Do we believe that the Spirit continues to call and shape the church?

"Very truly, I tell you," said Jesus, "the one who believes in me will also do the works that I do and, in fact, will do greater works than these because I am going to the Father."

Jesus spoke those words to his disciples before he went away from them. Who is listening now? There is no one but us; the body of Christ must claim space on the earth. "Do not let your hearts be troubled." We are not alone—you and I who dance and climb, who run and get knocked down, who lay on the grass and sit watching the late-night news. We are not alone. The Spirit of truth, the Advocate comes, surprising us at every turn saying . . . "Guess who?"

Questions for Meditation and Discussion

1. How do you define church?

2. What is the church's role in the world? Is this a "great time to be the church"?

3. How does the earliest Christian church provide a model for your church? How is it different?

4. Examine your own experience with church involvement over your lifetime. What caused any changes in your participation? What are you looking for in a church? Do you think you will ever find it?

5. Various reports inside and outside the church note that membership is declining in the twenty-first century. Perhaps your church experienced such a decline. What do you think are the reasons people are leaving church? What's happening in our society that may be contributing to this? Can such a decline be reversed? How?

6. Is the church still vital to society today? If so, how? If not, what would it take to make the church more vital to society?

7. In what ways should the church participate in culture? Should it incorporate culture fully, or should it remain completely aloof from culture; or is there a relationship in between these two?

8. **GROUP ACTIVITY:** Discuss various models of the church: church as institution; church as community (body of Christ); church as sacraments; church as herald; church as servant; church as school of discipleship. Based on your discussion of these models, how would you describe your church? Consider visiting other denominations as a group and comparing notes.

11 | Calling

What does it mean to be "called"? We often think of clergy persons as having received a call to the ministry or a call to preach. In some religious traditions, people are encouraged to embrace a religious vocation and to follow their calling. In seminaries, students are asked to share their call stories. Sometimes call stories are dramatic, pointing to a particular moment when the person "heard" a call from God to enter the ministry. Other times call stories are less dramatic: a person shares that God has spoken to them over many years, and that the accumulation of those "conversations" ultimately convinced them to embrace the call.

But the reality is that each one of us is called by God, whether as a layperson, a minister, a professional—in whatever way God has created us. Have we heard God calling us for a particular role or task or ministry? Are we really listening?

The Bible is filled with call stories. In these stories, some people are reluctant to accept the call, but others respond immediately. Perhaps the most well-known story is in Isaiah 6:1–9. The prophet describes his encounter with God: God is seated on a throne surrounded by heavenly creatures, seraphim, repeating the phrase, "Holy, holy, holy is the Lord of hosts." Isaiah responds to this vision by proclaiming that he is a man whose lips are not clean and who thus cannot speak for God to the people. In a dramatic scene, a heavenly creature touches Isaiah's lips with a burning coal, blotting out Isaiah's sin. Then, when God asks, "Who will go for us?" Isaiah responds in now familiar words, "Here am I, send me."

In the Gospel of Mark, Jesus calls his disciples to give up their daily work and to follow him. Jesus calls his followers "immediately" as he walks along the shore of the Sea of

Galilee, and they drop what they're doing to follow Jesus. Jesus's own call story is a little more dramatic, but he also accepts his call immediately and sets out to fulfill his God-given vocation. In Jesus's case, his baptism by John opens the heavens to Jesus's call: "Just as he was coming up out of the water, he saw the heavens torn apart and the Spirit descending like a dove on him. And a voice came from heaven, 'You are my Son, the Beloved; with you I am well pleased'" (Mark 1:10–11). As the story goes, Jesus "immediately" went out to make disciples and embark on his mission.

What is your call story? How does it develop? Are you even aware of it yet? As some sermon excerpts in this chapter point out, you do not need to be a minister or work in a church to be called by God. You might be called to be a preschool teacher, a truck driver, an engineer, a doctor, a social worker, a manager at a restaurant, a cook, or a librarian—or even to use those skills for kingdom purposes. How do we describe our calling to others? What is God calling us to do in our lives and in our work? How do you relate your calling as a Christian to your vocation?

The *Day1* preachers in this chapter provide inspiration to ponder as we consider the meaning of God's call on our lives.

"Clarity about Your Calling"

Joanna M. Adams • February 12, 2006 • Exodus 3:1–15

Here's a question for you: How do you decide about your life direction if you do not have a brother who comes back from the dead to tell you what to do? Ethicist Andy Fleming at Emory's Center for Ethics suggests that you could ask yourself three questions:

> What do I like to do?
> What am I good at? and
> What needs to be done in the world?

Where those questions overlap is what Fleming calls your "sweet spot," the place where you and I are meant to be and where we are able to live out our destiny at its fullest. I believe that there is not a single person listening to whom God has not spoken, some way, somehow, about where God wants you to go, what God wants you to do in the next chapter of your life.

How does God speak? Sometimes God's voice is heard in the form of an "A" in your favorite course in college. Sometimes God can speak through the "F" as well. Here's the deal: God has not left you alone to find your way. The question is whether or not you and I are listening to the ups and the downs in our lives, listening to the people around us who believe in us, listening to the surprise developments that come, truly, out of nowhere.

I do not know what you do in the world, whether you teach or work in an office, whether you are at the beginning of your career or whether you are retired, but I do know this about you: If your only goal in life is to get your needs met or to get the glory for yourself, then I will guarantee that you will miss out on the life God intends for you. The purpose of human life has always been about being a part of that which is larger and more enduring than one's self.

Friends in Christ, the life you're living now—it is the only one you've got. Don't spend it being scared, not being ready, not being what you should be. The bush is burning. It burns for you.

"A Fisherman for Jesus"

Micah T. J. Jackson • January 26, 2020 • Matthew 4:12–23

When two people are just getting to know one another—imagine they've just met at a party or something—a common question is, "What do you do?" And for a lot of us, what we do for work is (for better or worse) an important part of who we are. Interestingly, people don't usually ask me that when we first meet. You see, as an Episcopal priest I often wear a clerical collar, which many people recognize and marks me as a member of the clergy. They don't need to ask.

I imagine it was the same with Simon, called Peter, and his brother Andrew. But it wasn't their special clothes that gave them away. Indeed, if you met them on the street, their clothes were likely to be pretty utilitarian, maybe still wet from the sea. They would shake with rough hands, and the unmistakable odor of fish would accompany them. You wouldn't have to ask to know what kind of work they did. They were fishermen, no doubt about it. And in the time and place they lived and worked, that was all you needed to know about them—at least at first.

For the last fifteen years or so I've worked in theological education, mostly teaching in seminaries, but also ministering in congregations. And in that time I've seen hundreds—no, probably actually thousands—of people respond to the simple instruction Jesus gives in our passage: "Follow me!" Simon and Andrew were fishermen, but in my life, I've seen him say it to college students, bankers, police officers, full-time moms, philosophy professors, all kinds of people.

They almost always respond to Jesus in the same way: "Nah, I'm good!" They somehow have an instinctive feeling that Jesus is calling them away from the life they have. They don't want, or at least are not yet ready, to leave it behind.

I can't really blame them. After all, that's what I said the first time Jesus called me. And if we're being honest, the second and third time too, at least. And you know, it's not just people called to professional ministry who can tell this story. It's people who have heard the call to missionary work, or who have been invited to join the governing board of their congregation, or to tutor young children at the nearby elementary school, or even sing in the choir. They hear Jesus's voice somehow pulling them toward something new—"Follow me"—and yet their reaction is, "Nah, I'm good." They just don't want to, or are not yet ready to, take on this new way of living into their faith.

And that makes sense. The new is often scary, and as humans we've worked hard to achieve whatever peace and security we have, and of course we want to protect it. The Bible is full of stories of people who have said "yes" to God, and look where it got them. Hunger and rejection and sleepiness nights and prison time and beatings and death. "Nah, I'm good" is starting to sound like the most reasonable response.

So, what was going on with Simon and Andrew? What made them leave their nets and follow Jesus when, surely, they were subject to all the questions and worries any of us would be? And what about James and John, the sons of Zebedee? Why did they leave their boat and their father "immediately" and follow this strange man? They left it all to follow Jesus into an unknown future, all because he said, "Follow me."

But, of course, that's not all he said, is it? We don't often think about the second half of Jesus's call, but it seems to me that it makes all the difference. Jesus says, "Follow me, and *I will make you fish for people.*" This is a different kind of call, one that I think is easier to follow, and one that is actually more authentic to the kinds of calls that Jesus is offering us today.

You see, in Jesus's call to Simon and Andrew, he calls them not to abandon all that they know, but rather to put what they know at the service of the gospel. Jesus is saying that he has a new mission for them, a totally new kind of work, Kingdom work, but he is still going to need them to be fishermen. Something in their new calling will be an extension of their old calling.

For Peter and the disciples who were fishermen, maybe they saw the work of evangelism in fishing terms. They thought about going where the people were, throwing out the net of the Good News, and then hauling in the catch. The other disciples probably thought differently. For them, maybe bringing souls into the church was like collecting taxes, or vine dressing, or whatever work it was that they did before. Entirely different in some ways, but in some ways, very familiar.

When Jesus calls you to follow him, he doesn't do it because you've been wasting your life, or because he doesn't value what you have been doing until then. No, Jesus calls us to follow him precisely because of what we have been doing, and who we have become. Jesus knows how to use your skills, your gifts, your desires, and even your wounds, in deeper relationship and service to the One who is the maker of all plans.

And when people see you then, they might still assume you're just a fisherman—at least at first—but you will be so much more than that. In reality, you are a beloved child of God, uniquely gifted, and called by the Holy Spirit to serve the world in Christ's name.

"Choose to Care or Else"

Stephen Lewis • November 21, 2010 • Jeremiah 23:1–4

What does God care about? Jeremiah suggests that God mostly cares about the people of God and especially leaders who care for them. The prophet notes that caring for God's people is done in a way that enables them to flourish: *be fruitful and multiply.* And caring for God's people is not dependent on what they do or do not do. Rather, the act of caring is a reflection of what we value, what really matters to God.

What does caring for the people of God look like in practice? It looks like leaders who choose to create a space—a pasture—to develop rather than neglect and destroy God's people's sense of call. To ask provocative questions that connect rather than scatter God's people from a call to an abundant life together. To reflect on God's covenant with Israel that draws rather than drives God's people away from God's blessings and healing work in the world. And to establish opportunities that nurture the individual and collective vocation of God's people to be fruitful and multiply and to perpetuate God's blessings for generations to come, so that all the families of the earth shall be blessed.

Ultimately, our choices have either positive or negative consequences. We can choose to care for what God cares about or not. However, Jeremiah is certain that the Lord will attend to those of us who have not lived up to our capacity to be good stewards of what has been entrusted to us. The prophet infers that God will raise the next generation of shepherds—pastoral leaders—who will care.

So what is at stake for those of us in congregations, denominations, and theological institutions? What does Jeremiah invite a church in transition to care about? What are those of us who love the church called to do? Jeremiah advises that you and I are called to care about

God's sheep and the next generation of leaders who will care for them. We are called to choose.

When we don't choose to care for what God cares about, we undermine the promise God made with our ancestors to be fruitful and multiply. We threaten the everlasting covenant that was made between God and our fore-parents to be builders of nations, exceedingly fruitful, and the womb of future leaders who will emerge. We reduce the likelihood of young people hearing and responding faithfully to God's call in their lives. We cease to be the image and the presence of God in our communities. We no longer have an authoritative presence in the world.

Therefore, we must choose to care about an emerging movement to raise leaders, care for God's people, and bless the world. Choosing to care requires great courage. Choosing to care about what God cares for may lead us to let go of many things that occupy our time and attention. This is an invitation to take stock in what you and I really care about and what really matters to God.

Like the autumn wind, we hear the sound of this invitation whistling throughout our country in our organizations, theological institutions, denominations, and congregations. This invitation calls us to choose now what is possible. Choose now to suspend business as usual and imagine a church where God's people and leaders can be fruitful and multiply. Choose now to care less about what's popular and in your own best interest and instead consider the well-being of God's people, aliens, orphans, and widows. Choose now to exercise your denominational and congregational authority to change church processes that encumber the next generation of pastoral leaders from serving. Choose now to make theological education affordable and create new models for educating the next generation of shepherds God is raising up.

And if congregational pastures are not vital and healthy places where God's sheep and the next generation of shepherds can serve and care for each other, then we must choose now to change the conditions of these pastures so that God's people and leaders can live and thrive until David's righteous branch comes.

Until that time, the future of the church and of our children's children demands nothing less from you and me. We must choose this day what we really care about, because in the beginning God chose that we also might choose. And the ability to choose is what makes us most like God or not. Choose to care, or else.

"What's My Life?"

Kimberleigh Buchanan • February 1, 2004 • Jeremiah 1:4–10

We have trouble relating to Jeremiah's call. He was called to be a prophet to an entire nation. And a vast majority of us have not been called to be a prophet to the nation. Most of us haven't even been called to the ministry. So what does Jeremiah's call have to do with us?

I have been called to the ministry. I've been called to pastor a church, but I'm not the only person in my church community who has a specific calling from God. I see it over and over, people claiming their calls by God:

> Calls to work with youth or preschoolers or older adults.
> Calls to attend to the church's physical facility—thank
> goodness for those.
> Calls to work with the finances of the church.
> Calls to work not only in our church community but
> outside the church.
> Calls to work with the homeless and the hungry and
> refugees, and with the earth.
> Calls to be good accountants and bankers and teachers
> and doctors.
> Calls to be good moms and dads and grandparents and
> neighbors.

There is not one person in my church community or in yours who has not been called by God. All of us are known by God. All of us have been called by God to specific tasks. God will supply everything we need to fulfill our callings. And when we do fulfill our callings, when we live our lives, not only will it be good for us, but it will be good for the whole people of God. Now, that will preach, won't it?

Just live the life you are called by God to live. And many of us until the last couple of years were doing just that. We were happy in our jobs; we were living the lives God called us to live, and then the rug got pulled out from under us. The economy soured, our savings evaporated, our jobs disappeared, and suddenly we found ourselves unemployed or underemployed. And all of our time and all our attention of necessity turned to survival. Trying to live the life God has called you to live seems like a luxury when you're spending your time simply trying to live.

We are all known and beloved of God. We are all called by God to specific tasks, regardless of our circumstances. God will supply everything we need to fulfill our calling. And when we live our calling by God, it will be good for us, but it will also be good for the whole people of God.

"An Out-of-Order Lesson Calling Us to a New Day"

Michael Sullivan • June 5, 2011 • John 17:1–11

"Holy Father, protect them in your name that you have given me, so that they may be one, as we are one."

Why this lesson from John's gospel today on Ascension Sunday? It's out of order. Jesus is praying the High Priestly Prayer *before* his crucifixion. There's not a single reference to the resurrection here. Not one. What's the point of this out-of-order gospel? Well, the point is that Jesus was serious when he called you and me. We know that call is paramount to discipleship; we fill our churches with all kinds of programs and curricula to help us identify, understand, and respond to God's call.

But over the last fourteen years of my life in the church, the conversation about call has changed. And the conversation most of us are having is not pretty. This less than attractive discussion begins with a survey of the American religious landscape. Statistics from the Pew Charitable Trust, Gallup Poll, or Hartford Seminary tell us many things about the church, things we don't want to hear. For these think tanks tell us that the call is no longer experienced by a majority of Americans. Fewer and fewer people have any affiliation with a community of faith, and mainline denominations are shrinking at a rate that calls the future of these churches into question, all of them accounting for less than twenty percent of the population. The stats are hard to hear. The picture they paint is not affirming. But what these studies actually tell us is less about the death of the church and more about the future of it.

I'm sure when the disciples heard the High Priestly prayer, they turned to one another thinking, this is not what we signed up for, this is not why I left my nets upon the shore, this is not why I have left my family. Hearing Jesus's words, accepting that the difficult hour had come, those were not words of comfort but words of change, accompanied by the fearful unknown.

The beauty of this out-of-order gospel proclaiming the cross in the midst of our season of resurrection—the beauty comes raging right back into our lives, right back into our calls when we hear Christ's words once again. If we merely heard this prayer before Good Friday, we might mistakenly hear it for that day alone, for that appointed time. But on this side of the prayer, on this after-Easter day when we go back and listen once again, we hear the whole prayer and realize that what starts as Christ's obedience to change ushers in our obedience to change.

The point of Jesus's plea today is not his obedience to the past; the point is Jesus's obedience for our future. This is not merely a prayer that Jesus throws up into the heavens so that his work on the cross might be fulfilled. No, this prayer, heard on this side of Easter, is a prayer for you and me, for the church, that we might realize the faith Christ has in us, the faith Christ has in our call.

We may have faltered. We may have made every conceivable mistake at being one as Jesus and the Father are one. We may have so messed up that indeed the world begins to see us only as a hierarchical assembly of dressed up, religiously educated out-of-touch holy rollers. We may indeed be just as the news describes us.

Thanks be to God for this out-of-order prayer. Thanks be to God that Jesus is still praying for us. And thanks be to God for those who hold us accountable. May we hear all their voices and, once again, accept our call.

"Our First Calling"

Julie Pennington-Russell • September 7, 2008 • Mark 1:16–20

The point is that Jesus finds us, calls us, and the call is to go with him. This is about committing to the person of Jesus Christ. It's not about committing to a doctrinal statement or a program or some denominational tradition—it's about personal commitment to Christ. Jesus never said, "Come, be a Christian," or "Come, embrace this philosophy," or "Come, do this ministry." He said, "Come with me, belong to me, follow me."

I think that when most of us think about the issue of "our calling," we automatically think of something we're supposed to do or some career God may be asking us to take up. And some of us—let's be honest—get a little chewed up about this, maybe even a little frustrated that we don't have a better sense of what we're supposed to be about. "Lord, why don't you show me what you want me to do? What's my calling? How can I find it?"

But here's the thing: the Bible itself is amazingly un-anxious about all of that. For us one calling comes first. Give yourself to the person of Jesus Christ. Know him, follow him, love him, listen for him. And in doing that, you and I will find a huge freedom to do what we do best, to do what we love best. But see, that's not the main thing. Our first calling is to belong to Christ.

And isn't that good news? For one thing, if our first calling is to belong to Jesus, this gives us a huge freedom to change along the way—to grow and to become. You read the Bible and it becomes clear that Jesus has no investment in putting anybody in any kind of vocational straight jacket. Who among us doesn't just assume that the shape of our calling—the details of how we're going to lean into our one-and-only life down here—is going to change over the next ten, twenty, forty years? We can never predict how our lives are going to unfold.

So I wonder, if Christ is calling you and me today—and he is, because his calling comes fresh every day—what might you and I need to leave behind in order to get up and go? To follow Jesus means to be changed, to move on, to leave some things behind. When Jesus says, "Follow me," and we say, "okay," we never can predict where that's going to lead us. It's alright not to be sure of what it all means and how it'll all work out. All that matters is that Jesus has seen you as you are, has loved you, and has called you to follow.

Questions for Meditation and Discussion

1. How do you define vocation, or calling (*vocare*)?

2. What is the difference between a *career* and a *calling* or vocation?

3. What has God called *you* to do? Has that changed over your lifetime? Do you sense a new calling coming? Is there something you've always dreamed about doing but have never been able to—yet?

4. How would you describe the moment of your calling? Or, how would you describe the moment you decided to follow your calling and embrace a certain vocation?

5. What does it mean to you to be called to be a Christian? To be called as part of the body of Christ in the world? How does this calling affect your life?

6. What is the relationship between baptism and calling?

7. Do you feel as if you are doing what you truly have been called to do? Does your daily work truly reflect your calling?

8. **GROUP ACTIVITY:** There are many call stories in scripture: the call of David, the call of Isaiah, the call of Jeremiah, the call of Ruth, the call of Jesus, the call of various disciples, just

to name a few. Choose three or four of these stories, divide into small groups—each of which will read one of them—and talk about the similarities and differences in the stories. What biblical story most closely resembles your own call story? Share your responses with the whole group.

12 | Joy

In the beloved television special, *A Charlie Brown Christmas,* Linus reminds his friends of the true meaning of the day by reciting a familiar portion of Jesus's birth story from the Gospel of Luke: "Behold I bring you good tidings of great joy, for unto you is born this day a Savior, which is Christ the Lord."

When Linus finishes his words, the gathered group—which moments before had been angry with Charlie Brown for bringing a scrawny Christmas tree to their pageant—follows Charlie Brown home and surrounds him, singing "Hark, the Herald Angels Sing." The angry moment before Linus recited these words is transformed to a joyous celebration, reminding us all of the joy of the season, the joy of Christ's birth, and the joy that comes with the in-breaking of a new order in the world.

It's a joy that we can experience every day.

The joyous tidings that the angels share with the shepherds making their way in a frightening world is hardly the first time we hear about Jesus bringing joy to the world. In Luke 1, when Zechariah learns that his wife Elizabeth, described as "barren," will bear a child named John, he is at first "terrified." However, an angel tells him, "you will have joy and gladness, and many will rejoice at his birth." Later in the story, Mary, who is also pregnant, visits Elizabeth. When she sees Mary, Elizabeth exclaims, "Blessed are you among women, and blessed is the fruit of your womb. And why has this happened to me, that the mother of my Lord comes to me? For as soon as I heard the sound of your greeting, the child in my womb leaped for joy." The gospel begins in joy, even before Jesus is born.

It's a joy that we can experience every day.

For a story that begins with such joy, a momentary joylessness quickly overtakes it. Jesus brings joy and hope to many through healings and radical actions and teachings, but his followers are not always convinced of his identity, nor are they always joyful in their discipleship. Peter especially enacts his own joylessness when he denies that he has ever known, let alone followed, Jesus. When the world turns dark at Jesus's death, his followers flee in desperation, their hope broken—joyless. They must have felt deserted and completely bereft, wondering when the joy and hope they felt in following Jesus would return.

Jesus's death is not the end of the story, as we know, and his resurrection revives the joy of his followers. At the very end of the Gospel of Luke, when the risen Christ appears to his followers and blesses them, the followers "returned to Jerusalem with great joy, and they were continually in the temple blessing God."

This too is a joy we can experience every day.

But do we feel the same joy the earliest followers of Jesus felt? Can you recall the joy you felt when you first started following Jesus? How often do you feel that joy today? Where do you find joy in your daily life? If you are feeling joyless, how do you recover and restore joy to your life? How does your faith bring you joy, and how do you demonstrate the joy of your faith to others?

The *Day1* preachers in this chapter explore various facets of joy and offer nourishing moments of insight into the role of joy in our faith and lives.

"Should This Sermon Make You Happy?"

Scott Black Johnston • November 4, 2012 • Psalm 30

Why do people go to church? Why do they embrace religion? Why do they listen to religious radio programs like *Day1*?

Down through the centuries, Christians have articulated all sorts of different reasons for belonging to a faith community. In some settings, people have spoken, first and foremost, about church being a place where you can search for God, find a personal Savior, or at least learn the content of the Christian faith. Others emphasize their connection to a community of love and support. Still others point to liturgy, to their thirst for the sacraments, the music, and the prayers.

In every age, there have been those who have expected church to provide a moral compass for themselves or their children. Yet, others indicate that they have sought out church because they long to be part of a prophetic community—a group dedicated to meeting human need: feeding the hungry, caring for the poor, reaching out to a broken world with love.

In recent years, though, a large number of Christians give a different reason for associating with church, for having faith. Simply put, an increasing number of people hope that faith will make them *happy*. This motive for tossing back the covers on Sunday has uniquely American roots.

Barbara Ehrenreich wonders if our American obsession with having happy thoughts has dulled our common sense. Aren't negative thoughts important? Don't we wish, Ehrenreich asks, that more people, in analyzing recent real estate markets, felt nervous, pessimistic even, in the face of the belief that prices were on an eternal climb? In our urge to find the silver lining in even the darkest cloud, are we overlooking storms that could do us harm?

Maybe. Although our emphasis on positive thinking in this country doesn't seem to make us less anxious, less worried. Even though we are exercising our right—thank you, Thomas Jefferson—to pursue happiness, statistics indicate that Americans are the most anxious people on the planet. We consume over two-thirds of the world's anti-depressants. These pharmaceuticals have done wonders for many people, but they reveal something else, something basic. As a society, we think that there is something wrong with us—something that needs to be corrected—if we don't feel happy, leading some psychologists to ask, Are we putting too much pressure on ourselves to think positively—to be happy—all the time? That's a good question.

As people of faith, we may want to take a step back and ask, Is happiness really a Christian virtue? Does God expect us to be happy? Can church—can faith—make you a happier person?

The world is convinced, my friends, that happiness is humanity's chief goal, but God would have us go deeper. God prepares us for *joy*.

In Psalm 30 the writer says to God, "Hey, when I was prosperous, making the big bucks, I thought myself a self-made man, a happy camper, a hot ticket. I said out loud, I shall never be moved. Then everything fell to pieces. It literally went to Sheol—to hell. I was miserable. I was aching, God, mostly because I could not find your face."

Why are texts like this in the Bible? This passage is not unusual— not at all. If you were to toss out all the stuff that doesn't sound like positive thinking, you would have to do away with at least seventy-five percent of the Good Book. The Bible is crammed full of people speaking negative thoughts. It is kind of hard to put a positive spin on Jesus saying, "Take up your cross and follow me."

When we cover up the hard stuff in our faith, to proclaim a gospel centered in happiness and nothing else, we cheat ourselves. We miss the central message that the Bible goes to great lengths to convey: our God is not just the God of the happy, but the God of the suffering, the sad, the lost, the sick, the confused, and the downright angry.

When my mom died, my dad went into a tailspin. The television preachers that Dad once embraced didn't do it for him any longer. My brother and I couldn't seem to find the right words. Dad sunk deeper and deeper into depression. The local pastor, trying to toss my father a lifeline, recommended a grief group that met in the lobby of an old bank building in town. He never missed a meeting.

Finally, I asked him about it. "So, Dad, what's the grief group like?"

"Well," he said, "I have been so confused, so mad at God, and I didn't feel like anyone had any good answers. When I went to grief group, I found people who were like me. They taught me the primal scream. Do you know about the primal scream?"

"Yes, Dad," I said, "I know about the primal scream." It didn't seem like the kind of thing that my seventy-year-old father would be into.

"Well," he replied, somewhat sheepishly, "I have been doing it. I have been driving out past the Gunderson's farm to the crossroads there. I have been pulling over, and with the windows down. I have been doing the primal scream. And you know what?" he said. "I'm pretty sure God heard me."

God heard me. When Dad said that, it made me happy. No, scratch that; it gave me joy. God did not abandon me, says the psalmist. God heard me, and after the crying, the mourning, the sackcloth, the ashes, there was joy.

God, help us not to create an idol out of happiness. Help us to seek out the deep waters of faith and in those waves wash up in joy.

"Is There Joy in God's House?"

Thomas G. Long • March 21, 2004 • Luke 15:25–32

The house of God—the place where God and people meet—is a place of joy. But there are many of us for whom the word *joy* is not the best description of our faith. We think of ourselves as faithful people. We're willing to defend our faith and maybe even argue for it. It gives us guidance for living but it seems more like a responsibility, an obligation, than a deep joy. Some people even feel condemned by religion—judged, shunned, shamed. So as for the intense, freeing, overflowing, exhilarating, life-changing sense of joy—well, if the house of God is a house of joy, we cannot always say, "I was glad when they said unto me, 'Let us go into the house of the Lord.'" Why is this so?

Wherever God is, there is joy in the house. The House of God is a place of joy because it is there that people discover that what matters in life is not what they get but the grace they are given. It is there that people learn that what matters about them is not how high they climb, but how deeply they are loved by God. Isn't it strange that so many of us who are committed Christians stay outside the house of joy? Like the older brother in Jesus's third story. "What's that noise?" he said. "It's a party," replied the servant, "a joyful party. Your brother is home!" "A party for my brother? My brother who threw away my father's money? Foolish! A party for my brother who frittered away his life while I tried to make something of myself?"

I think part of what this is saying to us is that we will never really experience the joy of our faith until we realize that we are all outsiders who have been invited into the party of joy through no merit of our own. Some of us are like the younger brother, people who have wasted our lives, and some of us are like the older brother, people who have worked hard and who smolder with resentment because things are hard and responsibilities are heavy, and life is not fair. But the fact is, both are on the outside, both the younger son and the older son are on the outside, and it is God who invites us into the place of joy.

"Holy Laughter"

Samuel G. Candler • July 19, 1998 • Psalm 126; Luke 6:21

Somehow, a smile or a laugh is only valid to me when I know there has also been authentic struggle—when I know that the person in my company is not simply avoiding reality or offering cheap sentimentality. I believe in the smile of those who have suffered. "Blessed are you who weep now," said Jesus in Luke 6:21, "for you [shall] laugh." I believe in that kind of laughter. I believe in the beautiful smile of a woman who has been through labor and childbirth, not a sentimental smile, but one borne in pain.

I believe in the laughter of the matriarch Sarah, Abraham's old wife, beyond the age of childbearing. She was at the entrance to the desert tent while Abraham was showing hospitality to the three strangers who turned out to be—surprise—the Lord. After they ate, these strangers spoke as one. The Lord said that when he returned, Sarah would have a son. Sarah laughed to herself. It was a deep and lonely laugh, emerging from the weary feelings of forsakenness. She had ceased hoping now, she could only laugh. "After I have grown old, and my husband is old, shall I have pleasure?" What a ridiculous thought, perhaps even sacrilegious.

"Why did Sarah laugh?" the Lord asks Abraham. But Abraham does not answer. It is Sarah who then speaks directly for herself. She denies it. "I did not laugh." She was afraid now, sensing that she was in the presence of the almighty, the transcendent, someone who could—and would—change her life. I know that fear. It is a tremendous and fascinating mystery. "Oh," the Lord says, the voice of piercing truth and comforting mercy, "Oh, but you did laugh."

Oh, Sarah, you did laugh. And your laughter was "meet and right so to do," for it recognized the sheer absurdity of the Lord's way. The way of God is often so foreign to us humans that the most genuine way we can respond is to laugh. God's way takes us out of our ordinary worlds, into other orbits of wondrous flight and glory. Oh, Sarah, you did laugh. You were getting the joke.

And when the son is indeed born, what do Sarah and Abraham name him? They name him "Isaac." The word in Hebrew means "laughter." It means "someone laughs." I think it means everyone laughs. Our God is at work again, and God's way breaks into our human world like a great joke—something we know is true but which is also crazy and ridiculous and paradoxical.

God's business of redemption saves us no matter what circumstance we are in. Look at Psalm 126, written as the Hebrews were returning from exile and death, back into the promised land. "When the Lord restored the fortunes of Zion, we were like those who dream," the Psalmist says. "Then our mouth was filled with laughter, and our tongue with shouts of joy."

Such holy laughter is the sign that God has been at work again, bringing forth life from death. But two things must be present for that laughter to be holy. First of all, there has to be the experience of pain and emptiness—even death. Holy laughter is not the avoidance of pain. It must begin with authentic pain, an experience of some kind of death. Second, holy laughter emerges when that emptiness becomes filled with the grace and love of God.

For this reason, pain and suffering need not be the evidence that God has forsaken us. Instead, they are the fields, lying empty in winter fallowness, in which God will plant new seeds of spring hope. Your suffering and pain today is not the final word. The places where you suffer will be the very places where God will come alive. That is the gospel. That is the source of holy laughter.

I wonder if there has ever been a holy person who does not know how to laugh. For Sarah, her laughter was not so much an absence of faith. I believe her laughter was the first sign of faith. For she was beginning to get the joke. She realized immediately the absurdity of the thing. God bringing forth new life from her tired, old body. Laughter may be the first sign of faith, and people without faith are those who cannot laugh.

True reconciliation does not come automatically. It takes time and struggle and pain. But it does come. Reconciliation and grace come as sure as joy comes in the morning. So, laugh at the joke. God has reconciled the world to Godself through Jesus Christ. It seemed impossible once, and it may seem impossible again, but God has done it anyway. Laugh at the joke. Be reconciled to the fabulous, incredible love of God. Smile at Jesus. And smile at the people you live with.

"Living with Humor"

Harry N. Peelor • January 16, 1977 • Luke 7:31–48

What if the Lord of love doesn't deal with us in the same way we deal with our children? What if he can stand and see the stain of sin in our lives and still smile because he believes in the ultimate victory of righteousness? What if he can laugh at our evil because he's so confident of the goodness and love in God that cannot be conquered? Don't you want to walk with that kind of Lord? Couldn't you make that kind of Lord winsome enough so that somebody else could find him Savior, too?

This great Jesus with his sense of humor and perspective that keeps us from taking ourselves too seriously, or too lightly, helps us to discover ourselves, relax, and be ourselves. We can be in a whole new relationship with a Christ who has a sense of humor and who can laugh. And we can learn to laugh again and be the kind of people who will make it easier for others to be Christian.

Listen to the scripture and the wry humor of Christ as he says to the people: What in the world do you want? This generation is like some children in the marketplace. They complain that they pipe and you won't dance; they wail and you won't weep. John the Baptist came eating no bread and drinking no wine and you say that he is possessed by a demon. The Son of Man has come eating and drinking and you say, "Behold, a glutton and a drunkard, a friend of tax collectors and sinners."

What do you want from this Christ? He seems willing to rest the case in the consequences of human lives in their relationship with him. I truly believe that it was trivial to our Lord that he was criticized by the pious people as being outrageously shocking.

I am certain with some sense of humor, some deep laughter, he can promise you and me a relationship with him that will enrich our lives and the lives we touch. I think that is something that can spread a smile all through our being, and turn on in heaven the laughter of angels.

"Not Much but Enough for Me"

Stephen R. Montgomery • December 5, 2010 • Isaiah 11:1–10

The same vantage point I have as a pastor amidst tragedies and losses is also a vantage point on the new life that so often comes after. Every now and then I see a little shoot of life bursting forth from a dead stump. What seemed like the end of everything worth living for is being transformed before my eyes, in little tiny ways to be sure, even to the person it is happening to. But then, he or she does notice and—though still hurting—begins to take a step toward healing.

» A man who thought he could never risk loving again finds himself able to overcome his fear and opens himself up in a new relationship.

» A woman who has always equated security with a spouse discovers after a broken heart that she can make a home by herself and enjoy it.

» A man who cares for his invalid wife for a number of emotionally difficult years finds after her death that he has energy for the pursuits and interests he had almost given up.

» A woman who thought she could never enter a church again after her pastor told her to stay in an abusive relationship, because "that is her cross to bear," not only enters a church, but comes alive in its worship and mission.

» A couple that tried and tried and tried to have a baby with no luck. And then tried and tried and tried to adopt, with no luck. And then there's a baby, in Peru, and then several years later another baby from Nepal. I know this firsthand, my listening friends, for my son, born in Peru, is now in his second year of college. My daughter, born in Nepal, is now a senior in high school.

You get the picture. I could go on and on. Lives being lived out through Advent days of darkness and of unexpected light, these days of endings and of unexpected beginnings, these days of death and unexpected life. And the signs of all of these are not much: a shoot out of a stump, a branch out of the roots, a step forward, a smile—not much, but they are enough for me.

For every now and then, peace and joy break out in a place where I never would have believed it possible. Every once in a while, the deepest, oldest wound you can imagine actually heals. Every now and then, a hatchet gets buried so thoroughly that it is never dug up again. And I have no way of accounting for any of it except to say that it must come from above, Isaiah's vision—the light, the peace, the healing, the calm.

"The Gift of the Magi"

Mark Sargent • January 2, 2005 • Matthew 2:1–12

I can promise you that when the Magi experienced that joy in the presence of the child, they were struck by contrast. They were struck by how different that joy felt from the feelings they had experienced in that secret meeting with Herod. One felt so right; the other felt so wrong. The joy they felt when the star stopped was the inner confirmation that they had arrived at the place. Anytime we experience that kind of deep joy that is God's gift, then we know that we are where we are meant to be.

Have you ever had such a moment? Sure you have. Stop and call it to mind. A moment when things seemed to really line up for you. A moment when you felt so at home in your own skin, so at one with yourself and everything, that you knew the place at which you had arrived is the place where you belong. A moment when you can say, "This is me. This is why I'm alive. This is who I am. This is where I am meant to be." A moment when the star you've been following stops and you find yourself overwhelmed with the joy that comes from being you.

That's the moment I wish for you. That's the moment God wishes for all of us. And what I also wish for you is that all of your moments could be characterized by that kind of joy. In the new year to come and in whatever years may follow for us, what if all of life could be the delightful experience of being flooded by and overwhelmed with joy?

That joy happens when, like the Magi, we find ourselves at the place where we can freely and truly be who we really and truly are. Where is that joy place for you?

That's not as easy a question to answer as it may seem, because our lives are often not characterized by such joy. Our lives often reflect something other than the experience of being overwhelmed with joy. Why is that?

The Magi refused to go in the direction of their fears. Through the language of their dream, which is another way of saying that through their own God-given inner voices, they chose life and growth and joy. They trusted their own inner experience of joy, even if that experience flew in the face of the power and authority and expectations of the world. They went in the direction of the divine, even though Herod wanted them to go in another direction. They did that because that inner joy, the inner joy they experienced, is worth trusting and worth following and worth building a life around. That inner joy you experience when you're who and where you're meant to be is the still, small voice of God, beckoning you to live and move and have your being in the self God has given you, and not in what the world expects.

Herod has a thousand faces. He is alive today in anyone or anything that leads you away from being overwhelmed with the joy God wants you to have, the joy that comes from being who you really and truly are, where you really and truly want to be, and doing what you really and truly want to do. I know what it's like to capitulate to Herod. I also know what it's like to be flooded by joy. And I think I'm finally learning that any fear I have of Herod is not worth comparing to the delights of trusting my inner experience of joy that is the gift of God and moving courageously, confidently, in that direction.

That's what God wishes for you. I do know it's a tough move. Herod's pull is strong. But on this Sunday of Epiphany, when once again we watch a few stargazers offer some gifts to the child who is a king, perhaps we can recognize as well that the Magi bring a gift today to you and to me.

What they bring is the gift of their example. It's the example of saying *no* to Herod and *yes* to Christ. It's the example of saying *no* to fear and *yes* to joy. It's the example of saying *no* to the painful past and *yes* to the joyful future. It's the example of trusting your joy enough to build an entire life around it, whether the rest of the world understands and approves or not.

And if we can receive that gift, then, out of the experience of our lives joyfully lived, we will be more fully and richly able to offer our own gift to the Christ child. And I can think of no gift that would grace him more than for us to trust and to live each day in the joy that is the reason he came in the first place.

"Well, Here We Are"

Edmund Steimle • July 30, 1972 • Luke 15:11–13

One lovely summer Sunday in June we visited one of the prominent churches in New York in the morning and went to the Metropolitan Museum of Art in the afternoon. And the contrast in the two experiences was amazing. The service in the morning was about all one could ask for in a prominent East Side church in New York, I suppose. The music was good. The church was beautiful. The sermon was clear, intelligent, and pointed to the presence of the Spirit. The chanting was impeccable and the prayers include all of us there as well as those in need elsewhere.

But the visit to the museum was a delight, the paintings of Corot, Manet, and Rembrandt shimmering with color and vivacity and light—and above all, they were alive. It was sheer joy.

How come? How come you find light and life and vivacity and joy in a *museum*, of all places? And in the church of a summer Sunday morning—and not only in that church in New York, of course—you find all the proper ingredients for worship and yet a remarkable lack of light and life and vivacity and joy?

After all, the paintings were simply expressing what the painters had seen around them: the faces of people, landscapes, seascapes. Yet in church we were presumably celebrating the author and giver of everything around us, the faces of people, the land, the sea, and above all the love which holds it all together. And yet there was far more celebration and joy in the work of the painters than in the worship of the God who gave it all.

Perhaps you may say that I'm being unfair. I'm contrasting the work of some of the greatest painters of all time with the worship of ordinary people like you and me. Well, maybe so. But is it fair to suggest that a Christian celebration of God should reflect *something* of the wonder and joy and aliveness of life under God?

All this familiar story of the prodigal son is saying is that God wants to throw a party for us when the lost is found. When we've gotten sick and tired of trying to earn or deserve everything we get and just open ourselves to the joy.

And it is there. All around you. In the eyes of a love you don't deserve. In the aliveness and vivacity of a great painting. In the release that comes from knowing that we are recognized, accepted no matter who we are or what we've done. It's this outrageously generous love that wants to enfold us from the day we're born until the day we die— and even beyond that.

Maybe it might even creep into our worship on Sunday mornings if we're not careful—especially if we're not careful.

"Let's Dance"

Peter Wallace • July 15, 2018 • 2 Samuel 6:1–5, 12b–19;
Mark 6:14–29

Fitting in to get what we want in this world is usually rewarded by something no less awful than exactly what we wanted. And then by being used by someone else to get what *they* want.

But pure love, pure joy, pure devotion, pure openhearted, uninhibited worship of God never fits into this world. It exposes us, it makes us look foolish. It comes from a place where who we are, our naked self, is lovely, and it is offered without reservation. It breaks rules, and it often evokes resistance, even hatred.

The truth is, life is a dance. We're going to dance. All of us, whether we feel we have two left feet or have been trained for the ballet. The question is not whether, or even how we'll dance. It's *why*. Do we dance for the nefarious, scheming reasons Salome danced? Or do we dance for the pure, unadulterated joy of worship, opening ourselves to God and God's will, as David danced?

We dance every day in this world, in our interactions with our family, our loved ones, our coworkers, our neighbors, even strangers. We dance to the tune Jesus gives us, in worship, in seeking to fulfill his will for us in this life, in serving others wherever we may be.

Yes, we're all going to dance. Some of us will perform the steps better than others, but all of us can seek to dance joyfully, exuberantly, worshipfully, meaningfully. May God give us good reason—and courage—to dance with all our might. Right there in front of God and everybody.

Questions for Meditation and Discussion

1. How do you define joy? What is the difference between joy and happiness?

2. Do you experience joy following Jesus? Can you describe some of your most joyful moments as a disciple of Jesus?

3. When are the times you have felt you have no joy in your life or in your faith? How have you found joy?

4. Can you think of biblical passages that depict the joyfulness of Jesus and the joyfulness of his disciples?

5. Who are some biblical models of joy?

6. In his autobiography, *Surprised by Joy*, C. S. Lewis writes of the little moments of joy—he calls them "stabs of joy"— that appeared during his life, moments that could not be described in words. Can you recall the moments in your life you were "surprised by joy"?

7. How does your church encourage joyful worship? Where do you find joy in your worship or in your church community?

8. **GROUP ACTIVITY:** Choose three biblical texts from the sermons in this chapter and divide into three small teams of two or more. Have each team discuss the ways that joy is described in the text under consideration. As a larger group, listen to each team present these stories and then compare and contrast the ways that joy is described in each text. What do these texts teach us about the multi-faceted character of joy and the ways that it expresses out faith? Close by dancing the "Hokey Pokey."

APPENDIX

75 Years of Excellence in Preaching:
The Protestant Hour and *Day1*

Adapted by the Rev. Peter M. Wallace from a monograph by the Rev. Canon Louis C. Schueddig, D.D.

"Immortality: What Should It Mean to Us?" That is the title of the first *Protestant Hour* sermon broadcast on Sunday, April 1, 1945, five weeks before V-E Day. The preacher was E. T. Thompson, a Presbyterian professor of theology at Union Theological Seminary in Richmond, Virginia. Week after week since then, thousands of sermons have been preached on *The Protestant Hour*, which became *Day1* in 2002.

It all began when leaders of major Protestant denominations and educational institutions formed the Southern Religious Radio Conference near the close of World War II to spread the gospel through the popular medium of radio. The leaders represented the Southern Baptist,[5] Methodist, Presbyterian, Lutheran, and Episcopal denominations.

A Production Center for the Future

WSB Radio in Atlanta agreed to air the program from the very beginning, originally broadcast live from its studio, and continues to carry the program today as a public service. Soon other stations in the Southeast U.S. picked it up. The program was independently organized in 1950 by the Conference, and by 1953 *The Protestant Hour* was produced from a custom-built 68,000-square-foot building on the edge of the Emory University campus. It was called the Protestant Radio & Television Center (PRTVC).

---

5 The Southern Baptists participated only briefly, withdrawing in 1948 and moving their communications department to Fort Worth, Texas. The Cooperative Baptist Fellowship, a moderate group that left the SBC in 1991, has been represented on the program since 2003, along with the United Church of Christ and other mainline denominations.

In a time of massive growth in the mainline churches, the center was built for a promising future. It counted among its many features a massive soundstage in the basement for film and television production. As governor of Georgia, Jimmy Carter used the facility to practice speaking on television. Years later, President Carter would preach on a *Day1* program as part of a series on "Faith and Global Hunger."

Popular films such as *Driving Miss Daisy* were shot there. There were dressing rooms with showers, makeup vanities, and vaulted viewing stations with windows for producers and clients to observe filming. On each side of the V-shaped main floor were offices for staff and participating organizations. A chapel at the building's center was acoustically designed for sound recording and even had its own custom-made Schlicker pipe organ. Numerous university and church choirs recorded music for *The Protestant Hour* there, as well as record albums. With the new facilities, the radio program took a leap forward in production values and has continued to maintain the highest standards since.

By the 1970s *The Protestant Hour* had achieved national recognition, boasting a network of over 600 radio stations and the Armed Forces Radio Network worldwide. Because the Federal Communications Commission then required stations to air public service programming at no charge, *The Protestant Hour*—with its national and ecumenical scope—was ideal for stations to carry.

While the PRTVC was built for the future, that future was short-lived. By 2000 the brick building, across Clifton Road from the Centers for Disease Control and Infection on the Emory University campus, was full of mold, asbestos, and failing electrical wiring, and no longer functioned for emerging technologies. The building was sold in 2000 to Emory University and later demolished, the property redeveloped.

In early 2001 the radio program headquarters moved with its production partner the Episcopal Media Center, which maintained offices at the PRTVC for five years, to smaller space on the Midtown Atlanta campus of All Saints' Episcopal Church. In 2013 the operation moved to its current home on the campus of Second-Ponce de Leon Baptist Church in the Buckhead area of Atlanta.

The Primacy of Preaching

At the beginning, *The Protestant Hour* featured a different preacher each week, but by the 1950s the producers decided to feature one primary preacher year after year to represent their denomination. This approach not only built audience loyalty but also ensured sermon quality. It gave *The Protestant Hour* an enhanced reputation by presenting popular preachers such as Edmund A. Steimle, John A. Redhead, Robert E. Goodrich, Samuel Shoemaker, and many others, who would generally preach for one whole quarter of each year.

One thing that has bound the preachers together for all the decades of continuing broadcasts is their belief in the importance of proclaiming the gospel. This was summed up in a sermon on September 17, 1967, by George T. Peters of the United Presbyterian National Board of Mission:

> Preaching is a fantastic presumption. It is by preaching that Christianity is most conspicuously presented. Yet a pulpit-centered church is a dormant church. The only justification for a [preacher] standing in a pulpit is that the Lord of the church came preaching. The preacher's task is frightening and sometimes lonely. The gospel is not preached in a vacuum; it is preached in the world. We are all called to preach.

Many preachers in the first two decades had a vocal style distinctive of the times, with a formal and somewhat stilted manner. Others employed a more enthusiastic, dramatic approach. Some had distinctive accents—a Scottish brogue among some Presbyterians, or a British intonation from Episcopalians. Southern preachers spoke with a rich, syrupy drawl. One thing these early preachers rarely did, unlike today, was to share personal anecdotes or information. As the years went by this trend changed, as did the culture at large.

Engaging Important Themes in the 1950s and 1960s

The 1950s were in full swing by the time the program became established nationally. People were moving from rural areas to cities and from cities to suburbs. By 1960 a third of the country's population lived in the "'burbs." By 1951 the program had 140 stations in its network, and the coordinating producers changed their organizational name to the Protestant Radio Conference.

Amidst the social changes of the 50s and 60s, *Protestant Hour* preachers were late in coming to the issue of civil rights, while most never quite let go of the fear and threat of atheistic communism. Well into the 1960s atomic weapons and communism gripped many preachers' minds. They also agreed that moral decay was rampant within the country, rapid social change was causing problems in family life and society, and a lackluster laity burdened the church's efforts to share the faith of Christ.

Racism was mentioned early on and then disappeared for a decade. William H. Wallace Jr., a Methodist minister in Oklahoma City, proclaimed, "We need to be stripped of our prejudice.... The Southern Christian white man needs to take the lead in this great problem before our nation at this time" (February 9, 1947). Ten years later, on January 27, 1957, Herman L. Turner, a Presbyterian pastor in Atlanta, said, "We must speak the truth in love. Prejudice against persons on the grounds of race is contrary to the teachings of Jesus Christ. The racial tensions will be eased by those who are willing to begin by making themselves the instruments of our Lord's policy."

At the height of the Vietnam war and the protest movement, Edmund Steimle—who could sound both critical and affirming of what young people were doing—took a positive approach in his June 25, 1967, sermon:

> Thank God the young people of today with their long hair are willing to launch out into the absurd in the search for peace and justice. We will never know what Christ is up to until we are willing to obey in the face of the absurd command to follow, for example, to open up housing in our neighborhood to Negroes.

In fact, during this era it was Steimle more than any other preacher who made frequent reference to social problems on both a domestic and global level. He could lash out at popular culture, poverty, drugs, crime, and the comfortable pew that he thought too many churchgoers were occupying.

The hesitancy to speak of race relations ended abruptly in May 1968 with a series of sermons by preachers chosen by the National Council of Churches called *A Crisis in the Nation*. Diving right into the matter, Charles S. Spivey, executive director of the NCC Department of Social Justice, preached a sermon on June 16, 1968, called "Going to Hell." He said, "Angry black youth today are telling the church to go to hell. That is where it should go as it is separated from the sins of today. We need to deal directly with racism in our local church and neighborhood, in our club, lodge, or union."

As the program neared its second decade, there was a subtle shift as preachers chose themes such as marriage and family, the importance of Christian education, and the value of small and rural churches. One common theme was how to deal with personal suffering and anxiety. There was a consistent emphasis on a biblical text for the sermon—a reading or readings chosen by the preacher, rather than from a common lectionary as used by *Day1* preachers today.

Uniformly, the theology of *The Protestant Hour* sermons was in the neo-orthodox tradition. Yet, for all the scholarly background of those who preached on the program, nuances of theology were unimportant when it came to preaching the grace of God to a world in need. It was less important to be academic than to press upon the listener the importance of making that leap of faith, acknowledging Jesus Christ as the savior of the world whose grace alone is sufficient for salvation.

Powerful Voices in a Unique Pulpit

The Protestant Hour over the years had few real competitors. *The National Radio Pulpit* aired on NBC, and the *Lutheran Hour* was produced by the Lutheran Church-Missouri Synod and continues today. The Evangelical Lutheran Church in America aired *Lutheran Vespers*, later called *Grace Matters*, but ended production in 2009.

Alongside traditional Protestant religion in the media, a new evangelicalism arose in the 1950s led by Billy Graham, whose crusades aired weekly on television and whose radio program, *Hour of Power*, aired on numerous stations. In 1950, 49 percent of Americans were church members, but by 1960 the figure had jumped to 69 percent.

The program's success by the 1960s was due in no small part to the regularity of effective and engaging preachers such as Steimle, Redhead, Goodrich, and others regularly scheduled. Steimle had an ideal voice for the medium—rich and crisply resonant; listeners felt he was speaking directly to them. Redhead's delivery, like that of a beloved grandfather, magnetically drew in the listener. Goodrich had a rich Southern voice with near perfect elocution. There could be no better voices suited for the radio medium. Mixed with the brilliant and relevant content of their messages, these giants of preaching gave *The Protestant Hour* its standard of excellence. Truly this was the greatest preaching of the second half of the twentieth century.

Growth and Change in the 1970s

At the beginning of 1970 the *Protestant Hour* network had grown to 540 stations, with the Armed Forces Network carrying the program on all military bases, ships at sea, diplomatic posts, and commercial stations where there was a large U.S. military presence. Theodore Parker Ferris of Trinity Church in Copley Square, Boston, delivered the first series of the decade and was the first preacher to talk openly and personally about sex: "I grew up with total secrecy around sex. It aroused my curiosity. It also moved the whole thing out behind the barn. Sex is both powerful and dangerous" (March 1, 1970).

Music on *The Protestant Hour* took a turn in a modern direction by featuring popular, youth-oriented folk songs like "They'll Know We Are Christians by Our Love" and "Tell It Like It Is," in addition to traditional Protestant hymnody.

Edmund Steimle bade farewell on July 28, 1974, after twenty years of annual series. In this final broadcast he said,

> Every sermon is in part a prayer to the people to whom it is addressed. . . . I am grateful to you, the listeners, and for your letters and for putting up

> with me all these years and my fumbling, bumbling
> attempts to speak for God. We will need hope in the
> future. The world was rather tranquil when I started
> in 1955. And now the world is chiefly one of violence.
> You and I do know what the future does hold for us
> because of the truth of the resurrection. Praise and
> joy to you all in the years ahead.

He confessed, "For twenty years you're the only congregation I have had."

Though a Methodist laywoman preached early on, the first woman to preach a series on *The Protestant Hour* was Catherine Gonzalez, who alternated programs in the Presbyterian Series of 1975 with her colleague at Columbia Theological Seminary, Don Wardlaw. Their fifteen-week lectionary-based series was delivered as dialogue sermons.

A seminal moment in the history of *The Protestant Hour* came in late 1975 when the Presbyterian Church announced it would air a special Bicentennial Series with a different preacher, male, female, lay, and ordained, each week. The series, titled *The Pilgrimage of a People: One Nation Under God*, included Eugene Carson Blake, retired general secretary of the World Council of Churches, and two politicians, U.S. Senator Sam J. Irvin Jr. of North Carolina, famous from the Watergate hearings, and Governor Reuben Askew of Florida. The series also included Fred Rogers from the popular PBS children's program *Mister Rogers' Neighborhood*, who played and sang several songs on his program. Few knew at the time that Fred Rogers was an ordained Presbyterian minister. On April 24, 1977, Ruth Bell Graham, wife of Billy Graham, preached on "Why Have Homes?" She said, "The truly Christian home is the nearest thing to heaven we have on this earth. It is a place of refuge and restoration in a turbulent world." Ruth Graham was a child of Presbyterian medical missionaries in China and remained a member of the Presbyterian Church.

At the beginning of 1977 *The Protestant Hour* station network had grown to a peak of six hundred, in addition to the Armed Forces

Network, as a result of the FCC's Sustaining Time mandate for public service programming at no charge.

In June 1979 the United Church of Christ participated in *The Protestant Hour* for the first time, with James R. Smucker, minister of the New York Conference of the UCC, preaching. After this first series their participation was intermittent until they returned on a more regular basis in 2002.

Each year almost from the program's beginning, the denominational publishing houses, Cokesbury and John Knox Press, published the sermons of United Methodist and Presbyterian preachers. The Episcopal and Lutheran series were made available in pamphlets that could be obtained by mail or telephone through the PRTVC. The books helped reach people in cities and towns where *The Protestant Hour* was not heard on radio.

Challenges and Opportunities in the 1980s

Unfortunately, deregulation of the broadcast industry in the early 1980s led to a slow yet steady decrease in the number of stations in the *Protestant Hour* network.

The year 1980 marked the thirty-fifth anniversary of *The Protestant Hour*, and PRTVC staff and denominational producers decided to broadcast the best sermons from the past, which included C. S. Lewis presenting what would become his popular book *The Four Loves*. Lewis had recorded his then-unpublished work in the late 1950s in a hotel above Paddington Tube Station in London on a hand-carried reel-to-reel tape recorder with oversight by director Caroline Rakestraw. She suggested so many editorial revisions to Lewis's text that he later reported to his secretary he had found her "quite amusing." The classics also included Edmund Steimle, John Redhead, John Stone Jenkins, Robert E. Goodrich, Thomas L. Jones, J. Wallace Hamilton, and an original program produced for this series by Episcopal layman George Gallup Jr. of the polling organization.

The Episcopal Series for 1984 featured another classic C. S. Lewis work, *Mere Christianity*. Renowned actor Michael York, rather than

Lewis, read the text that had originally aired on BBC Radio during World War II.

On April 22, 1984, Barbara K. Lundblad began sharing the Lutheran Series with John Vannorsdall and would eventually take his place as the annual Lutheran voice. She was then serving as pastor of the Lutheran Church of Our Savior's Atonement in Manhattan. In 1997 she was appointed professor of homiletics at Union Theological Seminary. Barbara rapidly became a *Protestant Hour* icon and returned year after year as the ELCA preacher well into the current century. With her frequent references to growing up on an Iowa farm, Barbara was, and remains, a consummate storyteller, a deeply pastoral preacher, and extremely popular.

By then, it was not unusual for women to preach an entire twelve-week series. The Rev. Carol Matteson Cox, pastor of a church in the Bronx, New York, offered the United Methodist series for 1984. She dared speak of homophobia in her August 12 sermon: "In some areas of our lives all of us participate in the sin of overbearing pride. Perhaps the group most looked down on are homosexual persons."

A new conservatism erupted as many people in the pews grew suspicious of the supposedly liberal national church headquarters, whose budgets they felt should be cut and repurposed to local churches. Many pointed a finger at national leaders for their progressive stances on issues related to race, peace, gender equality, the environment, hunger, and HIV-AIDS. This trend would eventually lead to the elimination of denominational funding for the program in the mid-2000s.

The first African American to offer an entire twelve-part series in the 1980s was the Rt. Rev. John T. Walker, Episcopal Bishop of Washington, DC. Born in Barnesville, Georgia, and brought up in Detroit, Walker was also the first African American to be admitted to Virginia Theological Seminary in 1951. He earned a world reputation for social activism and was a good friend of Archbishop Desmond Tutu.

One of the best-known preachers of that generation, named by *Time* magazine as "the prince of the Protestant pulpit," preached the Presbyterian Series in 1987. David H. C. Read, pastor of Madison

Avenue Presbyterian Church in New York City, preached a stunning series that pushed boundaries. A Scottish Presbyterian, he had served as Her Majesty's Chaplain in Scotland. When he died, his *New York Times* obituary described Read as taking "an outspoken approach to controversial issues with a showman's verve to the pulpit in one of New York's most prominent churches." He served at Madison Avenue Presbyterian for thirty-three years.

Having gained a national reputation as one of the finest moderate Southern Baptist preachers and authors, John Claypool felt called to become an Episcopal priest. With his warm, resonant voice he drew people to God everywhere he preached. Claypool first preached on *The Protestant Hour* in late 1988. He plumbed spiritual depths with words that one can hang on to for a lifetime. For example, "By choosing not to love, one is assured of never having to suffer" (September 25, 1988).

As the 1980s came to a close, *Protestant Hour* sermons remained mostly personal in their overall tone and message. William K. Quick, pastor of the Metropolitan United Methodist Church in Detroit, said in his February 26, 1989 sermon, "The church today is filled with people who outwardly reflect peace and contentment but whose hearts cry out for someone to love them just as they are: lost, confused, frustrated, sometimes frightened, guilty, and often unable to communicate even with their families."

More Changes in the 1990s

For the church, the 1990s represented the climax of a long period of mistrust of national church headquarters. The issue of human sexuality was particularly divisive, and the ordination of women, now settled in all the mainline churches at a national level, had not yet won full acceptance in local congregations. *Protestant Hour* preachers for the most part chose to avoid dealing with these hot topics that were tearing the church apart. They stayed with biblical themes with personal, inspirational explication of the texts. Since the four participating denominations funded *The Protestant Hour* from national budgets, the program's future was in real peril.

By the 1990s the program had unified with an opening theme song, a contemporary version of "A Mighty Fortress Is Our God," and Don Elliott Heald—who had served as announcer for the Episcopal series for decades—became the host for all the programs; before his retirement in 1999, his voice had been heard on the program for five decades. He was succeeded as host by Rick Dietrich, a Presbyterian minister on the faculty of Columbia Theological Seminary. Longtime announcer Sherrie Miller, a former WSB Radio program host, began serving in the late 1990s, and Donal Jones began recording, producing, and editing the program, continuing today as director of audio and video production.

By the 1990s, the inherent "Southernness" of the program and the lack of women preachers had ended. On July 8, 1990, Barbara Brown Taylor preached for the first time on *The Protestant Hour*. Her series aired before she was named "one of the top twelve preachers in the English-speaking world" by *Time* magazine. Barbara, associate rector at Atlanta's All Saints' Episcopal Church at the time, had just completed her first book, *The Seeds of Heaven*, which she read as her sermons on *The Protestant Hour*.

In mid-1992 a major change in the program format occurred when the producers decided to stop airing one preacher or one denomination for a straight twelve weeks or so, but rather to feature a different preacher each week on a rotating basis among denominations, in order to create a more ecumenical environment. Preachers were asked to use the Common Lectionary as the basis of their sermons, since all participating denominations now followed it. The decision also arose in part because busy church pastors no longer had the time to prepare a dozen sermons for the program; they were now asked to preach three or four programs at the most, rotating with other preachers.

In 1996, as the World Wide Web came into public consciousness, *The Protestant Hour* developed a website that included program audio files and transcripts. In the years since, the website at Day1.org continues to expand its faith-building resources. A podcast version of the program has been offered through iTunes since the late 1990s and is now available on most podcast platforms.

A New Name, a New Day of Ministry

In 2000, the PRTVC board decided to sell the now decaying building on Clifton Road, get out of the landlord business, and focus on the radio program, whose affiliate roster had by then dropped to 130. The organization's name was changed to The Protestant Hour, Inc. Peter Wallace was hired in 2001 to revitalize the program, and together with the denominational producers he did so with new theme music, a new website, and in 2002 a new program name, *Day1*, which refers to the first day of the week, Sunday, and offers a hopeful, fresh invitation to hearing God's Word preached.

By the mid-2000s, despite affiliate growth to over 200 stations, denominational support had finally come to an end, and the Protestant Hour, Inc. merged with the Episcopal Media Center in 2004, reinventing itself as the Alliance for Christian Media. A new *Day1* Advisory Board composed of well-respected pastors, professors, and church leaders helped to promote the program to potential preachers, who now came from a much broader range of historic Protestant denominations including the United Church of Christ, Cooperative Baptist Fellowship, Christian Church (Disciples of Christ), National Baptist, American Baptist, Reformed Church in America, and others.

In 2005 host Rick Dietrich left to pastor a church, and Peter Wallace added hosting duties to his production responsibilities, expanding the program's opening interviews with the preachers and adding a follow-up segment to discuss the sermon.

Over the seventy-five years of weekly broadcasts that comprise the *Protestant Hour* and *Day1* archives, the messages journey through the times in which we lived and in which the preachers preached. World War II brought out the intense need for faith in fearful times, and the growth of Communism put the church on the defense against an atheistic political system that sought to dominate the globe. After those years, the programs never spoke so plainly and passionately about global issues facing our church and nation.

Modernity arose in the fifties with its incumbent problems of vast social growth, which led us to the sixties and the Vietnam War and youth movements and sensitivity training. The generation gap tore families apart, and churches found their memberships dropping. As life became more complex in the later decades of the twentieth century, *The Protestant Hour* always tried its best to offer a message of faith and hope, encouraging the listener to trust in God, pray for a deeper relationship with Jesus Christ, serve God in their daily lives, and know that no matter what comes our way, God's grace is sufficient.

That message remains the same in 2020, as the *Day1* radio program celebrates seventy-five years of ministry, now not only on the radio but via various podcast platforms. The consistency of message—the approach to biblical interpretation, the assurance of a God who can love us through our self-doubt, our suffering, our divorce or illness, and the challenge to follow Jesus in every area of life—has never changed. It is truly a testimony to the heritage of Protestant religion and those called by God through human speech to make these gospel truths known.

ABOUT THE PREACHERS

The authors of the excerpts in this book, representing the historic mainline Protestant churches, are some of the most effective preachers of the twentieth and twenty-first centuries. Their words come from transcripts of Protestant Hour *and* Day 1 *sermons.*

THE REV. DR. JOANNA M. ADAMS served as senior pastor of Morningside and Trinity Presbyterian churches in Atlanta and Fourth Presbyterian Church in Chicago. After retiring she was interim pastor of Atlanta's First Presbyterian Church. She is a founder of Higher Ground, an interfaith group based in Atlanta.

THE REV. DR. M. CRAIG BARNES is the president and professor of pastoral ministry at Princeton Theological Seminary. Earlier he was a professor at Pittsburgh Theological Seminary. He served pastorates in Pennsylvania and Wisconsin and at the National Presbyterian Church in Washington, DC. A frequent lecturer and preacher, he is the author of eight books.

DR. DIANA BUTLER BASS is an author, speaker, and independent scholar specializing in American religion and culture. She consults with religious organizations, leads conferences, and teaches and preaches across the country. Her best-selling *Christianity for the Rest of Us* was named as one of the best religion books of 2006 by *Publishers Weekly* and won the Book of the Year Award from the Academy of Parish Clergy.

THE RT. REV. NATHAN BAXTER was the bishop of the Episcopal Diocese of Central Pennsylvania for eight years before retiring in 2014. He is professor of practice at Lancaster Theological Seminary. He earlier taught in three other seminaries and served parishes in Pennsylvania and Virginia. He was dean of the National Cathedral in Washington, DC, from 1991 to 2003.

THE REV. BETH BIRKHOLZ went with her husband as co-pastor to Holy Cross Lutheran Church in Livonia, Michigan, in 2017, after serving churches in Colorado and Georgia. She is now manager of congregational engagement for the Southeast Michigan Synod of the ELCA.

THE REV. BOB BOHL was moderator of the 1993 General Assembly of the Presbyterian Church (USA). He served churches in Kansas and Florida and was chairman of the board of the Presbyterian Publishing Corp. Retired in 2003, he continues to serve congregations as an interim pastor.

THE REV. EMILY M. BROWN, ordained in the United Church of Christ, is pastor of First Reformed Church, Hastings-on-Hudson. Earlier she served as associate pastor of Broadway United Church of Christ in New York City. She is on the board of Young Clergy Women International and co-managing editor of "Fidelia," their online publication.

THE REV. DR. MICHAEL BROWN was a United Methodist minister in North Carolina before becoming senior minister of Marble Collegiate Church (Reformed Church in America) in New York City, from which he retired in 2018. He is the author of six books. In 1995, he was included in the "Great American Preachers" book series.

THE REV. DR. WALTER BRUEGGEMANN is widely considered one of the most influential Old Testament scholars and theologians of the last several decades, and an important figure in modern progressive Christianity. He is professor emeritus of Old Testament at Columbia Theological Seminary, Decatur, Georgia, and has authored numerous books.

THE REV. DR. KIMBERLEIGH BUCHANAN is senior pastor of First Congregational United Church of Christ in Asheville, North Carolina. She earlier was pastor of Pilgrimage UCC in Marietta, Georgia, for sixteen years.

THE REV. DR. THOMAS LANE BUTTS, a popular speaker and preacher, is minister emeritus of First United Methodist Church in Monroeville, Alabama. Author, columnist, and friend to beloved novelist Harper Lee, he served United Methodist churches in Florida and Alabama for many years.

THE VERY REV. SAMUEL G. CANDLER is dean of the Cathedral of St. Philip, Atlanta. He earlier served churches in Georgia and South Carolina, where he was dean of Trinity Cathedral in Columbia. He has served on liturgy and music committees in several dioceses. He writes a commentary called "Good Faith and the Common Good."

THE REV. DR. ANNA CARTER FLORENCE is the Peter Marshall Professor of Preaching at Columbia Theological Seminary in Decatur, Georgia. She is a frequent speaker and lecturer at churches and conferences including the Festival of Homiletics. Her writing is included in numerous journals and she is the author of several books, including *Preaching as Testimony*.

BISHOP KENNETH CARTER is bishop of the Florida Conference of the United Methodist Church. Prior to his election as bishop in 2012, he was pastor of churches in North Carolina. Author of several books, he is the president of the Council of Bishops of the UMC.

THE REV. DR. JOHN CLAYPOOL (1930–2005), highly regarded for his preaching and writing, served Southern Baptist and then Episcopal churches in Kentucky, Tennessee, Georgia, Texas, Mississippi, Alabama, and Louisiana. He served for fourteen years as rector of Saint Luke's Episcopal Church in Birmingham, Alabama. He was also professor of homiletics at Mercer University McAfee School of Theology in Atlanta.

THE REV. DR. MARTIN COPENHAVER, ordained in the United Church of Christ, served as president of Andover Newton Theological School. He retired in 2019. Earlier he served churches in New England and Arizona. He has written numerous books, columns, and articles.

DR. COURTNEY COWART served in the recovery of Ground Zero from historic St. Paul's Chapel. She was co-director of the Office of Disaster Response for the Episcopal Diocese of Louisiana after Hurricane Katrina. After serving as director of the Beecken Center and associate dean at the School of Theology of the University of the South, Sewanee, Tennessee, she became executive director of the Society for the Increase of the Ministry.

THE REV. SUSAN CROWELL, engaged by Trinity Lutheran Church in Greenville, South Carolina, for a one-year internship, stayed on to serve as associate pastor. She has been senior pastor there since 2001. She has served the S.C. ELCA Synod in several executive and governance positions.

THE MOST REV. MICHAEL B. CURRY was installed as presiding bishop and primate of the Episcopal Church in 2015. Earlier he served as bishop of the Episcopal Diocese of North Carolina for fifteen years. Ordained in New York, he has served parishes in North Carolina, Ohio, and Maryland.

BISHOP ANDREA DEGROOT-NESDAHL served two terms as bishop of the South Dakota Synod of the Evangelical Lutheran Church in America, 1995–2007. After retirement she worked on an ELCA special project to eradicate malaria and an awareness project for AIDS.

THE REV. ROBERT DUNHAM was senior pastor of University Presbyterian Church in Chapel Hill, North Carolina for 26 years. He retired in 2017. He served churches in Alabama, Georgia, South Carolina, and New York. He is the author of *Expecting God's Surprises: Devotions for the Advent Journey*.

THE REV. DR. ALEX EVANS is pastor of Second Presbyterian Church in Richmond, Virginia. He served churches in South Carolina and Virginia, and as chaplain with the Blacksburg, Virginia Police Department. He is convening director of the Virginia Law Enforcement Assistance Program, which offers support and counsel to law enforcement officers in Virginia.

THE REV. JOE EVANS is senior pastor of First Presbyterian Church in Marietta, Georgia. He earlier served churches in Georgia and Tennessee. He has been an editor of the *Lectionary Homiletics* journal since 2005.

THE REV. DR. WILLIAM E. FLIPPIN JR. is assistant to the bishop and director of evangelical mission for the Southeastern Pennsylvania Synod, ELCA. Previously, he was the first African American pastor of Emmanuel Lutheran Church, the largest multi-racial Lutheran congregation in Atlanta.

THE REV. DR. CHRISTOPHER GIRATA is rector of Saint Michael and All Angels Episcopal Church in Dallas. Previously he served as rector of Calvary Episcopal Church in downtown Memphis, Tennessee, in parishes in Alabama and Maryland, and at the National Cathedral in Washington.

THE REV. DR. LARRY GOODPASTER is bishop-in-residence at Candler School of Theology at Emory University in Atlanta. He served the United Methodist Church in the Mississippi Conference and the Alabama-West Florida Conference. He became bishop of the Western North Carolina Conference in 2008 and upon retirement in 2016 assumed the position at Candler.

THE REV. DR. J. BENNETT GUESS is executive director of the American Civil Liberties Union of Ohio and a prominent civil and human rights activist. He formerly served as vice president of the Council for Health and Human Service Ministries, in the United Church of Christ national organization, and as a local church pastor for twelve years.

THE REV. CANON SCOTT GUNN serves as executive director of Forward Movement, a ministry of the Episcopal Church to inspire disciples and empower evangelists. He is on the board of the *Anglican Theological Review*. An honorary canon at Christ Church Cathedral, Cincinnati, he previously served congregations in Rhode Island.

THE REV. DR. DAVID P. GUSHEE is distinguished university professor of Christian ethics and director of the Center for Theology and Public Life at Mercer University in Georgia. One of the foremost Christian ethicists in the world, he is the author or editor of over twenty books, including *Moral Leadership for a Divided Age*.

THE REV. DR. HOMER HENDERSON is retired after twenty years as pastor of the Claremont (California) United Church of Christ. He also taught at Claremont School of Theology. A UCC minister and the first ecumenical appointee of the United Methodist Church, he served churches in Connecticut, Texas, and Kansas.

THE REV. CHRISTOPHER HENRY is senior pastor of Second Presbyterian Church in Indianapolis. He earlier served as pastor of Shallowford Presbyterian and at Morningside Presbyterian in Atlanta. Upon graduation from Columbia Theological Seminary in 2007, he received the seminary's highest academic honor.

THE REV. JAMES NEIL "DOCK" HOLLINGSWORTH JR. is senior pastor of Second-Ponce de Leon Baptist Church in Atlanta. Earlier he had an eighteen-year career with Mercer University, serving at McAfee School of Theology as assistant dean and assistant professor of leadership.

THE REV. DR. JAMES C. HOWELL, senior pastor of Myers Park United Methodist Church in Charlotte, North Carolina, is also adjunct professor of preaching at Duke Divinity School. He has written twelve books, including *Yours Are the Hands of Christ*.

THE REV. JUAN CARLOS HUERTAS is pastor of First United Methodist Church in Houma, Louisiana, a congregation that is part of the Bread or Stones Campaign dedicated to improving the lives of children in the state. He earlier was pastor of churches in Shreveport, Baton Rouge, and Ragley, Louisiana.

THE REV. DR. MICAH T. J. JACKSON is president of Bexley Seabury Seminary Federation in Chicago. Earlier he served as the Bishop John Hines associate professor of preaching and director of comprehensive wellness at Episcopal Seminary of the Southwest. He is the author of the forthcoming *Preaching Face to Face: An Invitation to Conversational Preaching*.

THE REV. DR. KATHLYN JAMES was pastor of Edmunds United Methodist Church in Edmunds, Washington, until her retirement in 2016. Earlier she served four United Methodist congregations in the Pacific Northwest, including First United Methodist of Seattle from 1999–2007.

THE REV. DR. SCOTT BLACK JOHNSTON is senior pastor of Fifth Avenue Presbyterian Church in New York City. He previously served as pastor of Trinity Presbyterian Church in Atlanta and is a former professor of homiletics at Austin Theological Seminary in Texas.

THE REV. L. BEVEL JONES III (1926–2018) was elected bishop in 1984, serving the Western North Carolina Conference of the United Methodist Church, after serving six congregations in the North Georgia Conference. Upon retirement, he came to Candler School of Theology, Emory University, as bishop-in-residence. He was a trustee of Emory and many other institutions and organizations.

THE REV. DR. THOMAS L. JONES has worked as ambassador-at-large for Habitat for Humanity International since 2005. Earlier he was senior pastor of large Presbyterian congregations in Kentucky, Florida, and Maryland. He served as vice president for a theological seminary and as a faculty member at two seminaries.

THE REV. ALEX JOYNER, superintendent of the Eastern Shore District of the Virginia Conference of the United Methodist Church, has served appointments in England, Texas, and Virginia. He was campus minister at the United Methodist Wesley Foundation at the University of Virginia. He is the author of a vocational discernment curriculum for young people, *Where Do I Go Now, God?*

THE REV. DR. PATRICK KEEN, ordained in both the Baptist and Lutheran traditions, is a trained congregation developer. He served as pastor of Our Savior's Lutheran Church in Milwaukee, Bethlehem Lutheran Church in New Orleans, and several other Chicago-area congregations, until his retirement. He has been a leader in civil rights, anti-violence, and interfaith causes.

BISHOP LEONTINE KELLY (1920–2012), a Methodist trailblazer, was the second woman and the first African American woman elected to the Council of Bishops in the United Methodist Church. Among Kelly's many contributions to the denomination was as a founding member of Africa University, the first Methodist university on the continent of Africa.

VICTORIA LAWSON, a student at Mercer University McAfee School of Theology, has served as children's ministry intern at Wieuca Road Baptist Church in Atlanta and in various roles at Brookwood Baptist Church in Birmingham, Alabama. She is also a volunteer with Young Life.

C. S. LEWIS (1898–1963), British writer and theologian, wrote more than thirty books that have been translated into more than thirty languages and sold millions of copies. "The Chronicles of Narnia" have been popularized on stage, TV, radio, and cinema. His books, including *The Four Loves* and *Mere Christianity*, are appreciated by Christians from many traditions.

THE REV. DR. KAROLINE LEWIS holds the Marbury E. Anderson chair in biblical preaching at Luther Seminary. She previously taught at Candler School of Theology, Columbia Theological Seminary, and Augsburg College. She is the author of a commentary on the Gospel of John and *SHE: Five Keys to Unlock the Power of Women in Ministry*.

THE REV. KRIS LEWIS-THEERMAN is associate rector and director of children, youth, and family formation at St. Bartholomew's Episcopal Church in New York City. After being a stay-at-home mother, full-time student, and professor, she was ordained and earlier served parishes in Massachusetts, Connecticut, and New York.

THE REV. STEPHEN LEWIS has worked with the Institute for Church Administration & Management and as a teaching assistant in the Black Church Studies Department at Candler School of Theology. After serving as president of the Forum for Theological Exploration, he assumed the interim presidency of Interdenominational Theological Center in Atlanta. He is ordained by the American Baptist, National Baptist, and Progressive National Baptist churches.

THE REV. DR. THOMAS G. LONG, ordained in the Presbyterian Church (USA), is the Bandy professor emeritus of preaching at Candler School of Theology at Emory University, Atlanta, and earlier taught at Princeton and Columbia Theological Seminaries. He is the author or editor of over a dozen books on preaching and worship. He was named one of the twelve most effective preachers in the English-speaking world by Baylor University.

THE REV. DR. BARBARA K. LUNDBLAD is the Joe R. Engle professor emerita of preaching at Union Theological Seminary in New York City. She served sixteen years as a parish and campus pastor and has taught preaching at Yale Divinity School, Princeton Seminary, Hebrew Union College, and the Association of Chicago Theological Schools. A longtime *Protestant Hour* and *Day1* preacher, Lundblad is the author of *Transforming the Stone: Preaching through Resistance to Change* and *Marking Time: Preaching Biblical Stories in Present Tense.*

THE REV. GARY MANNING is rector of Trinity Episcopal Church in Wauwatosa, Wisconsin. He earlier served churches in Florida and Virginia. He frequently serves as consultant to churches working with clergy and leadership. He was the 2009 recipient of the John Hines Preaching Award given by Virginia Theological Seminary.

THE REV. DR. PETER W. MARTY is senior pastor of St. Paul Lutheran Church in Davenport, Iowa, and publisher of *The Christian Century.* He is the author of *The Anatomy of Grace,* as well as numerous articles on leadership, preaching, and parish renewal. He was host of the weekly national ELCA radio broadcast, "Grace Matters." In 2010, the Academy of Parish Clergy named him "Parish Pastor of the Year."

THE REV. PATRICIA MCCLURG (1939–2019) served churches in her native Texas and then on the Presbyterian Church (USA) General Assembly Mission Board for nine years, ultimately as its director. She was the only woman on the committee of ten that wrote "A Declaration of Faith," a document that continues to speak to worship and faith in the Presbyterian Church (USA). In 1988–89, she served as the first clergywoman president of the National Council of Churches.

THE REV. DR. LAURA MENDENHALL was president of Columbia Theological Seminary in Decatur, Georgia, from 2001 to 2009. She earlier served churches in Florida and Texas. Now retired, she is a senior philanthropy advisor for the Texas Presbyterian Foundation.

THE REV. DR. STEPHEN R. MONTGOMERY retired as senior pastor of Idlewild Presbyterian Church in 2019, having served there since 2000. He earlier served churches in Kentucky and Georgia. He teaches at Memphis Theological Seminary.

THE VERY REV. KATE MOOREHEAD, dean of St. John's Episcopal Cathedral in Jacksonville, Florida, is a well-known speaker and author. Her book, *Healed: How Mary Magdalene Was Made Well,* is a biblical and theological perspective on mental illness.

THE REV. DR. MARGARET NEILL (1939–2013) was one of the first African American women ordained as a priest in the Episcopal Church. She served for many years in the diocese of Western Michigan, then led parishes in Arizona and North Carolina.

THE REV. DR. JOHN PHILIP NEWELL is a poet, peacemaker, scholar, and minister in the Church of Scotland. He is internationally acclaimed for his work in the field of Celtic spirituality. Formerly warden of Iona Abbey in the Western Isles of Scotland, he divides his time between writing in Edinburgh and teaching on both sides of the Atlantic.

THE REV. DR. DOUGLAS OLDENBURG was president of Columbia Theological Seminary, Decatur, Georgia, from 1987 to 2000. He was moderator of the 210th General Assembly of the Presbyterian Church (USA). In 2018, he received the Award for Excellence in Theological Education, the highest honor in the PCUSA for those who teach, lead, and support theological education.

THE REV. HARRY N. PEELOR (1922–2011) was the founder of Christ United Methodist Church in Pittsburgh. His career included stints as chaplain to the Pittsburgh Steelers, motivational speaker to the Air Force, and director of outreach ministries for Guideposts Associates, which specialized in evangelism through inspirational stories.

THE REV. JULIE PENNINGTON-RUSSELL is senior pastor of First Baptist Church of Washington, DC. In 2007 when First Baptist Church of Decatur, Georgia called her as senior minister, it was the largest church associated with the Southern Baptist Convention or Cooperative Baptist Fellowship to call a woman as senior minister.

THE REV. DR. WILLIAM K. QUICK (1933–2017) was senior pastor of Metropolitan United Methodist Church in Detroit. Quick was also associate general secretary of the World Methodist Council, a visiting professor at Duke University Divinity School, and the coordinator of Partner Churches in Latvia and Lithuania.

THE REV. SHARI L. RATES is pastor of Metropolitan United Methodist Church in Rome, Georgia. Before entering Candler School of Theology at Emory University, she spent five and a half years in Micronesia, where she worked with children and youth through the Peace Corps. She has served in leadership roles and in several congregations in the North Georgia Conference.

THE REV. DR. CHARLES REEB became senior pastor of Johns Creek United Methodist Church in 2018 after serving churches in Georgia and Florida. He teaches at Candler School of Theology. He is the author of several books, including *That'll Preach! 5 Simple Steps to Your Best Sermon Ever.*

THE REV. DR. FRED ROGERS (1928–2003), American television personality, musician, puppeteer, writer, producer, and Presbyterian minister, was the creator and host of the preschool television series "Mister Rogers' Neighborhood," which ran from 1968 to 2001. *Won't You Be My Neighbor?* is a 2018 documentary film about his life and guiding philosophy.

THE REV. ASHLEY ROSSER WILSON preached on *Day1* as a Forum for Theological Exploration fellow and student at Candler School of Theology at Emory University. She now serves as director of mission for United Methodists of Greater New Jersey.

THE REV. DR. DEBRA VON FISCHER SAMUELSON became senior pastor of Lutheran Church of the Good Shepherd, Minneapolis, in 2010 after serving on the pastoral staff of Lutheran Church of the Redeemer in Atlanta for eight years. She retired in 2019.

THE REV. MARK SARGENT is a retired United Methodist minister. From 1979 until 2010 he served as pastor of several congregations in the North Georgia Conference, including as the founding pastor of Wesley United Methodist in Augusta and the senior pastor of First United Methodist in Rome, Georgia.

THE REV. DR. WILLIAM L. SELF (1932–2016) was founding senior pastor of Johns Creek Baptist Church, Alpharetta, Georgia, from 1991 to 2012, and senior pastor of Wieuca Road Baptist Church from 1964 to 1990. A leader in the Cooperative Baptist Fellowship, he taught at Mercer University McAfee School of Theology. He also served as board chair of the Alliance for Christian Media, producer of *Day1*.

THE REV. DR. OZZIE E. SMITH JR. is founding senior pastor of Covenant United Church of Christ in South Holland, Illinois. He serves as adjunct professor of ministry and D.Min. advisor at McCormick Theological Seminary, on whose board he serves. The Memphis native is known for his phenomenal jazz saxophone playing.

THE REV. SUSAN SPARKS is senior pastor of Madison Avenue Baptist Church in New York City—the first woman in its 160-year history. A former trial attorney, she is a stand-up comedian whose work has been featured in *The New York Times, O (The Oprah Magazine),* and on ABC and CNN. She is the author of *Laugh Your Way to Grace, Preaching Punchlines,* and *Miracle on 31st Street.*

THE REV. DR. EDMUND A. STEIMLE (1907–1988) was professor of homiletics at Union Theological Seminary and taught at Lutheran Theological Seminary in Philadelphia and Louisville Presbyterian Seminary. He also served as a Lutheran pastor in Massachusetts and New Jersey. He was one of the most popular *Protestant Hour* preachers, preaching for a quarter of each year for twenty years.

THE REV. KEVIN STRICKLAND was elected bishop of the Southeastern Synod of the Evangelical Lutheran Church in America in 2019. Earlier he served in the churchwide office in Chicago since 2014, including a stint as the assistant to the presiding bishop, executive for worship of the ELCA. He earlier served churches in Tennessee and South Carolina.

THE REV. DR. MICHAEL SULLIVAN became president of the Kanuga Conference and Retreat Center in North Carolina in 2016. Earlier he was rector of Holy Innocents' Episcopal Church in Atlanta.

THE REV. BARBARA BROWN TAYLOR is a bestselling author, teacher, and Episcopal priest. She served on the faculties of Piedmont College,

Columbia Theological Seminary, Candler School of Theology at Emory University, McAfee School of Theology at Mercer University, and the Certificate in Theological Studies program at Arrendale State Prison for Women. In 2014, *Time* magazine included her on its annual list of Most Influential People. *Holy Envy*, her fourteenth book, was released in 2019.

THE REV. DR. DANIEL VESTAL, pastor of Peachtree Baptist Church in Atlanta, earlier served as the coordinator of the Cooperative Baptist Fellowship and as pastor of churches in Atlanta and Texas. He is distinguished university professor of Baptist leadership and director of the Eula Mae and John Baugh Center for Baptist Leadership at Mercer University.

THE REV. DR. WILLIAM H. WILLIMON is professor of the Practice of Christian Ministry at Duke Divinity School in Durham, North Carolina, where he returned after serving as the bishop of the UMC North Alabama Conference from 2004 to 2012. The author of dozens of books, he was earlier dean of Duke Chapel and professor at Duke University.

THE RT. REV. ROBERT C. WRIGHT is bishop of the Episcopal Diocese of Atlanta. Earlier he was rector of St. Paul's Episcopal Church in Atlanta, the oldest African American Episcopal congregation in the state. A Navy SEAL, he was canon pastor and vicar at the Cathedral of St. John the Divine, New York City.

THE REV. DR. BRETT YOUNGER is senior minister of Plymouth Church in Brooklyn, New York. For eight years he was associate professor of preaching at Mercer University McAfee School of Theology in Atlanta. Before that he served as a pastor for twenty-two years in Texas, Kansas, and Indiana. He is the author of *Who Moved My Pulpit?*

THE REV. ROBERT M. ZANICKY has been senior pastor of First Presbyterian Church in Wilkes Barre, Pennsylvania, since 1988. He also teaches at Misericordia University in the Religious Studies Department.

The editor, **THE REV. PETER M. WALLACE**, is executive producer and host of the *Day1* radio/podcast and internet ministry (Day1.org) and president of the Alliance for Christian Media, based in Atlanta. Peter is the author of ten books, including *Getting to Know Jesus (Again): Meditations for Lent*; *The Passionate Jesus: What We Can Learn from Jesus About Love, Fear, Grief, Joy, and Living Authentically*; *Connected: You and God in the Psalms*; and *Living Loved: Knowing Jesus as the Lover of Your Soul*. He is also the editor of the *Day1* youth and adult formation resource, *Faith and Science in the 21st Century: A Postmodern Primer* and *Heart and Soul: The Emotions of Jesus*. An Episcopal priest, he serves in the Diocese of Atlanta. His website is www.petermwallace.com.

HENRY L. CARRIGAN JR., writer of the *Day1 Faith and Science in the 21st Century* book, assembled the excerpts and wrote topic introductions.

ETHEL WARE CARTER researched and composed the preacher biographies.

THE REV. CANON LOUIS C. "SKIP" SCHUEDDIG, D.D., longtime executive director of the Episcopal Media Center and the Alliance for Christian Media, wrote the monograph upon which the historical Appendix is based. He is a graduate of Northeastern University and Virginia Theological Seminary, which also bestowed an honorary doctorate. Ordained a priest in 1973, he earlier served congregations in Illinois and Michigan, and was appointed an honorary canon of the Cathedral of St. Philip in Atlanta.